Cambridge Elements ≡

Elements in the Archaeology of Europe
edited by
Manuel Fernández-Götz
University of Edinburgh
Bettina Arnold
University of Wisconsin–Milwaukee

THE BELL BEAKER PHENOMENON IN EUROPE

A Harmony of Difference

Marc Vander Linden
Bournemouth University

European Association
of Archaeologists

CAMBRIDGE
UNIVERSITY PRESS

Shaftesbury Road, Cambridge CB2 8EA, United Kingdom

One Liberty Plaza, 20th Floor, New York, NY 10006, USA

477 Williamstown Road, Port Melbourne, VIC 3207, Australia

314–321, 3rd Floor, Plot 3, Splendor Forum, Jasola District Centre,
New Delhi – 110025, India

103 Penang Road, #05–06/07, Visioncrest Commercial, Singapore 238467

Cambridge University Press is part of Cambridge University Press & Assessment,
a department of the University of Cambridge.

We share the University's mission to contribute to society through the pursuit of
education, learning and research at the highest international levels of excellence.

www.cambridge.org
Information on this title: www.cambridge.org/9781009496889

DOI: 10.1017/9781009496872

First published 2024

A catalogue record for this publication is available from the British Library.

ISBN 978-1-009-49688-9 Hardback
ISBN 978-1-009-49686-5 Paperback
ISSN 2632-7058 (online)
ISSN 2632-704X (print)

The Bell Beaker Phenomenon in Europe

A Harmony of Difference

Elements in the Archaeology of Europe

DOI: 10.1017/9781009496872
First published online: February 2024

Marc Vander Linden
Bournemouth University

Author for correspondence: Marc Vander Linden,
mvanderlinden@bournemouth.ac.uk

Abstract: Covering vast swathes of Europe, the Bell Beaker Phenomenon has enjoyed a privileged status in the history of archaeology and is often referred to as a key period in the transition from the Neolithic to the Bronze Age partly due to the emergence of social élites. After a brief presentation of the historiography of the Bell Beaker Phenomenon, this Element offers a synthetic account of the available evidence structured on a regional basis. Following the renewed interest in human mobility generated by stable isotopes and ancient DNA studies, the central thesis developed here is that the Bell Beaker Phenomenon can adequately be described as a metapopulation, a concept borrowed from population ecology. This title is also available as Open Access on Cambridge Core.

Keywords: prehistoric Europe, Neolithic, Bell Beaker Phenomenon, population history, Bronze Age

ISBNs: 9781009496889 (HB), 9781009496865 (PB), 9781009496872 (OC)
ISSNs: 2632-7058 (online), 2632-704X (print)

Contents

Preface

Although written over a few months, it is appropriate to state that this Element has been in the making over the twenty years that have passed since I completed my doctoral thesis on the Bell Beaker Phenomenon. In the meantime, my take on archaeology has changed through the vagaries of short-term academic jobs and the serendipities of scientific meetings. At the same time, it is evident that the discipline I was trained in during the 1990s has evolved to become the multi-faceted topic I now teach at Bournemouth University. In many respects, the structure of this small Element, combining traditional synthetic sections with more speculative/hypothetical ones inspired by ecology, reflects this entangled personal and disciplinary trajectory.

Key themes here are those of connectivity and mobility. Under the impetus of new techniques, archaeology is coming to terms with its self-inflicted mistrust of human dispersal as a mechanism for change. Challenges in addressing questions of mobility and migration are now back at the forefront of archaeological thinking. From a personal standpoint, my involvement in these discussions has been coloured by fact that at the same time as Sr isotopes and ancient DNA were making their way into the archaeological toolbox, I became a migrant myself, having moved from Belgium to the United Kingdom. This new status was initially and will forever remain linguistic. Yet, being a migrant was, at least at the beginning, never really about identity. Over the past few years, however, the political climate in the United Kingdom has reshaped and even rephrased in strictly defined legal terms this migrant identity. How much these have effectively influenced my thinking on human mobility is unclear, but the realities of life always feature in one's personal evolution.

1 Thematic Encounters

1.1 Archaeological Cultures . . . Again – But Why?

The thought of writing an Element on an archaeological culture may sound old-fashioned in the early 21st century AD. These days indeed, one prefers to dedicate time, effort, and academic reputation to a process, a theme, a method, or a theory, but not to an archaeological culture, that old and reeking concept which has been lingering at the bottom of our toolbox for over a century. A sceptical reader may wonder if the author did not learn any lessons from sixty years of archaeological fashions, which all seem to agree that archaeological cultures survive only as oddities stacked on the shelves of a cabinet of archaeological curiosities. In my defence, I would argue that archaeological cultures remain relevant for contemporary and future archaeological method and theory. Their prominence within the so-called third revolution spear-headed by ancient DNA is surely telling; either the lure of high-profile publications is leading archaeologists to discard their theoretical heritage and pride or – not mutually exclusive – there might well be still some life left in the old concept for understanding the past. A very brief detour via the history of archaeological cultures can help to shed some light on the latter proposition.

Archaeological cultures were originally developed to organise the growing amount of data faced by antiquarians, and thus played a foundational role in the transition of archaeology from cataloguing to interpreting the past (Roberts and Vander Linden 2011). That they then became tangled in an obsessive focus on ethnic groups is as much a by-product of the intellectual ambiance at the time as a spontaneous consequence of their methodological and conceptual design. It is undeniable that archaeological cultures can easily be translated into faceless groups endlessly, almost haphazardly, migrating across Eurasia and other continents. But, as argued here and elsewhere (Roberts and Vander Linden 2011), their core analytical remit is still relevant to today's challenges. Arguably, most archaeological cultures were often merely monothetic entities defined through ceramic typology only, and there is a tempting parallel to be drawn here with the primacy given to ancient DNA data in recent narratives about past migrations. Beyond such cautionary tales, one of the key objectives of this Element is to show how archaeological cultures, as analytical tools, can help us to handle the fast-flowing streams of unstructured, proteiform data which increasingly characterise the archaeological record.

The subject of this Element, the Bell Beaker Phenomenon, provides a case in point. This near-consensual label refers to an uneven set of artefacts (namely the eponymous bell-shaped ceramic vessel, but also various artefacts possibly related to archery, as well as daggers and other copper implements), and practices (especially individual burial, often but not always linked to binary sex-related body disposal rules) widely distributed across the European space and beyond during the 3rd and, locally, early 2nd millennium calBC. The Bell Beaker Phenomenon stands proud amongst the behemoths of Holocene European Prehistory, those quasi-mythical analytical beasts that fascinate as much as they seem to resist any straightforward interpretations. Familiar names such as the Linearbandkeramik, Corded Ware, Urnfield, or La Tène should all bring back memories of introductory lectures taught in archaeology departments across Europe and beyond. Although most specialists would probably raise an eyebrow at contemplating the possibility of comparing these complexes, I would suggest that four common traits define access to this pantheon of archaeological complexes:

1) *Space* – All of these archaeological complexes present extensive spatial distributions, breaching modern-day boundaries and covering large swaths of the European peninsula. From a Bell Beaker point of view, its undeniable importance lies in its presence along the entire Atlantic European coast, from southern Scandinavia to the tip of the Iberian Peninsula and even northern Africa, and from the Irish shores to the banks of the Danube in central Hungary.

2) *Time* – This transgressive character is also temporal, as so-called cultural complexes often lie at the interface between broader chronological subdivisions (e.g., Mesolithic-Neolithic, Neolithic-Bronze Age, Bronze Age-Iron Age). Not only does the geographic Bell Beaker spread correlate with a varied linguistic terminology (e.g., French, Spanish and Portuguese *Campaniforme*, German *Glockenbecher*), this diversity also encompasses many chronological labels, including Late or Final Neolithic, Early Bronze Age, and Chalcolithic. Behind this myriad of names lies a tacit, common acknowledgement that the Bell Beaker Phenomenon is situated at the interface between the Neolithic and the Bronze Age. For many, this transition would not be merely chronological but testimony of a profound societal transformation from one historical epoch to another, marked by the rise of social hierarchies. Since the work of Vere Gordon Childe, various scenarios have considered the leading role of copper metallurgy in this process, although it is noteworthy that this particular technology, subject to uneven rates of production and consumption, had existed in various parts of Europe since the late 6th millennium calBC (Roberts et al. 2009). The link between early copper metallurgy and the Bell Beaker Phenomenon is thus tenuous at best, or at least very localised. More recently, some have revived the idea that new systems of belief and social institutions, introduced by migrant populations, were the key factor in propelling Europe into a new age (e.g., Kristiansen et al. 2017), although, as we will see, this particular hypothesis is not free of major difficulties either.

3) *Definitional uncertainty* – Cultural complexes exhibit wide-ranging variation in the archaeological record leading to unresolved and often Byzantine disputes amongst specialists as to what constitutes, or not, their material identity. Despite many attempts, there is still no agreement as to what represents a common artefact or package, let alone assemblage or practice, which would apply to and define the entirety of the Bell Beaker domain. At the risk of being pedantic, one could even argue that in light of the diversity of the archaeological record and the multiplicity of research traditions and approaches, all of the aforementioned local Bell Beaker labels are actually not strict synonyms and do not point to analogous archaeological units,

although, as will be argued further here (see Section 4), their exceptional combination is what makes them stand out in European later prehistory.

4) *Human dispersal* – As a correlate of their wide-ranging spatial distribution, debates have raged regarding the role of human migration in the making of these archaeological cultures, a theme whose vagaries are the most remarkable yet predictable aspect of the Bell Beaker historiography. After early years of emphasis upon the centrality of migration, followed by three decades of total denial, the Bell Beaker Phenomenon has become a laboratory for the application of new scientific techniques which led to the factual demonstration of some level of human mobility. The latest addition of ancient DNA has confirmed not only the existence of episodes of human dispersal but, as for all themes outlined above, a marked regional and temporal variation in the magnitude of these events across the Bell Beaker territory.

Taken together, these four traits allow us to map some of the interpretative challenges raised by the Bell Beaker Phenomenon. They also reinforce the thesis that the concept of archaeological culture still presents some validity: how do we account, on the one hand, for the fact that the Bell Beaker Phenomenon is perceived as a key transition period largely shaped by human dispersal, and on the other hand, it exhibits such a wide spatial distribution and range of material expressions? Rather than assuming the existence of a Bell Beaker archaeological culture, this constitutes one of the explicit research questions at the core of this element: is a definition, for instance expressed in polythetic terms (Clarke 1968), of the Bell Beaker Phenomenon possible, and if so, how does it help us in characterising the processes at play in linking together this panoply of records, practices, and human communities?

1.2 An Illustrious Gallery of Portraits

Unsurprisingly, these four defining traits regularly feature across the vast and long-lasting literature dedicated to the Bell Beaker Phenomenon. Perhaps more for this period than for any of the other archaeologically attested cultural behemoths, the historiography of the Bell Beaker Phenomenon is impressive and deceptive in equal measures. Impressive given its gallery of illustrious protagonists, including the likes of Vere Gordon Childe, Stephen Shennan, David Clarke, and, perhaps less well-known to a non-English readership but fundamental in their own right for European continental archaeology, Evžen Neustupný and Alain Gallay. And yet the range of scholars who have engaged with this topic is sadly deceptive as theories of the Bell Beaker Phenomenon have tended to be repetitive and explore a narrow range of themes. This is not to say that there is a lack of conceptual imagination, far from it, but that the majority of existing theories weave together the same transversal themes, ever repeated even if subject to fluctuations largely predicted by the wider trends of archaeological theory.

Culture-historical accounts are not merely defined by their focus on migration as the driving force of change but also in their insistence on the position of the Bell Beaker Phenomenon at the transition between the Neolithic and the Bronze Age, and on its extensive geographical distribution, the latter emphasis related to the need to anchor relative time through typological comparison. One of the earliest occurrences of the label 'bell beaker' was set forth by Abercromby (1902). The purpose of his contribution was actually to provide a typological framework and geographical origin for 'the advent of a people of new stock, distinguished from the older neolithic [*sic*] inhabitants by taller stature and moderately brachycephalous head' (Abercromby 1902: 374). Within several decades, Abercromby's lead was followed by several scholars across Europe, and the Bell Beaker Phenomenon quickly acquired the international stardom that characterises it to this very day. As comments and papers were published, the narratives gradually became more layered and complex, as the following excerpt from the sixth edition of Gordon Childe's opus magnum *The Dawn of European civilisation*, the epitome of the culture-historical take on the Bell Beaker Phenomenon, illustrates:

> *The Beaker-folk was a principal agency in opening up communications, establishing commercial relations, and diffusing the practice of metallurgy [...] Beaker-folk can be recognised not only by their economic activities but also by their distinctive armaments, ornaments and above all pottery, associated together everywhere in their graves. Indeed, the inevitable drinking cup, which gives a name to its users, may be more than a readily recognized diagnostic symptom; it symbolizes beer as one source of their influence* (Childe 1957: 222, 223). *The people buried with Bell Beakers [...] are round-headed [...] In this instance, therefore, it looks as if culture and race coincided and one might legitimately speak of a Beaker race* (Childe 1957: 227).

While some of Childe's vocabulary has aged poorly and may seem unfortunate to a modern readership, this quote is testimony to his genius and legacy, as it encapsulates all the major culture-historical tropes of the Bell Beaker Phenomenon: unquestioned association between the eponymous bell beaker ceramic vessel and a migrating human population, defined by specific physical (today genomic) traits, as well as with copper metallurgy, funerary weaponry, and the social practice of drinking.

The key topic remained for several decades the identification of a Bell Beaker homeland, a putative quasi-mythical geographically well-delimited land from which Bell Beaker material traits, and hence their historical interpretation, would flow. In hindsight, it is easy to consider such obsession as naive, an impression reinforced by the fact that, with the sole exception of Ireland and Britain – culture-historical Britain was always in a position of reception rather than innovation as famously pointed out by Clark (Clark 1966) – all regions within the Bell Beaker domain have at some point been considered candidates for the title of homeland (e.g., Clarke's oft-forgotten preference for Mediterranean France: Clarke 1970). This being said, two main contenders have battled for supremacy: on the one hand, various locations along the Rhine basin, and on the other hand, the Iberian Peninsula, in particular the Tagus estuary. Christian Jeunesse recently provided a thorough account of the evidence, and lack thereof, supporting this latter hypothesis (Jeunesse 2015). In a nutshell, while it is undeniable that the Portuguese Atlantic façade has provided some the oldest radiocarbon dates associated with Bell Beaker traits (Section 2), a key issue remains the absence of clear typological prototypes for several facets of the Bell Beaker archaeological record. This limit was recognised by early 20th-century scholars, who handled it with sometimes impressive technical sophistication. In a contribution which marks the nadir of the culture-historical tradition, Edward Sangmeister suggested that the Bell Beaker variation was best explained by an initial movement out of the Iberian Peninsula towards central Europe, followed by a later backflow in the opposite direction, thus suggesting the existence of two distinct, successive homelands (the so-called Rückstrom theory: Sangmeister 1966). Sangmeister's work rested upon an exceptional command of the then available documentation (though not free of flaws: Clarke 1970), but the elegance of his argument ultimately lies within what remains a narrow perception of the archaeological record.

While Sangmeister was drawing arrows criss-crossing Europe, the first series of ^{14}C dates of Bell Beaker contexts were carried out in the Netherlands (de Vries et al. 1958). While this revolutionary technique provided the means to test independently competing hypotheses about the location of the Bell Beaker homeland, its impact on the field would not be noticeable for nearly two decades. In the late 1970s, building upon the legacy of early radiocarbon dates and previous typological work (van der Waals and Glasbergen 1955), Lanting and van der Waals published an influential study combining typo-chronology and absolute chronology and argued for the local development of Dutch Bell Beakers from the regional facies of the Single Grave Culture (Lanting and van der Waals 1976; Figure 1). While Lanting and van der Waals never explicitly considered the implications of their research for areas

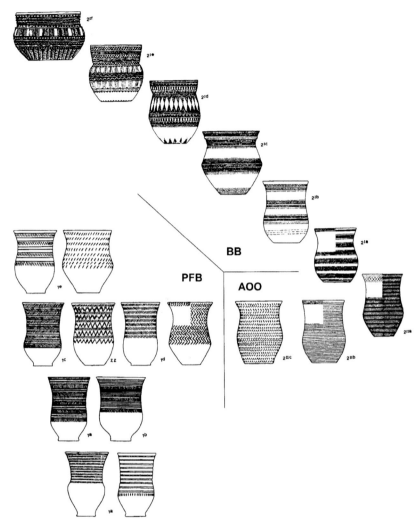

Figure 1 The 'Dutch model' of typo-chronological development
from the single grave culture to the Bell Beaker phenomenon
(after Lanting and van der Waals 1976).

outside the remit of their original case study, their work was soon embraced as proof of a homeland located in the Lower Rhine which offered a robust alternative to the Iberian hypothesis (e.g., Harrison 1980). Although the details and wider relevance of this typo-chronological scheme are still discussed, it is noteworthy that the general validity of the local Single Grave Culture – Bell Beaker sequence remains unquestioned (Beckerman 2011–2; see Section 2).

As any student of archaeology knows, the late 1960s and 1970s witnessed a paradigm shift with the onset of processual archaeology and the contributions of larger-than-life figures such as Lewis Binford and Colin Renfrew. In the Bell Beaker case, a break from culture-historical themes is noticeable, but it took the form of a more uneven transition. For instance, if the Dutch model directly stems from the availability of radiocarbon dating, its impact remains limited to weighing more in favour of a given homeland than in any upheaval of the associated theoretical architecture. The intellectual development of the Cambridge-based scholar David Clarke provides a good example of this transition.

Clarke's doctoral thesis, completed in 1962 but only published in 1970, took advantage of emerging computing power to pioneer the application of statistical techniques to archaeological interpretation (Clarke 1970). His matrix analysis applied to an extensive corpus of British bell beakers allowed him to define several typological groups in a quantitative way. These groups had limited geographical coherence and, as their labelling indicates (e.g., Wessex/Middle Rhine), were all seen through the culture-historical prism as a direct reflection of cross-Channel contacts. Though featuring in *Analytical Archaeology* (Clarke 1968), this interpretation had little influence on the rest of this landmark publication in theoretical archaeology, and at the time of his premature death in 1976, Clarke's view on the Bell Beaker Phenomenon had changed radically. In line with his definition of an archaeological culture as a polythetic set, he considered the bell beaker as an artefact to be unrelated to any specific assemblage, but rather embedded in wider social strategies (Clarke 1976). Stephen Shennan, one of Clarke's students, furthered this view by demonstrating that various components of Bell Beaker material culture in central Europe did not fulfil the canonical definition of an archaeological culture, as their distribution was hardly overlapping (Shennan 1978). In contrast, Shennan defined a stable assemblage of artefacts found primarily in funerary context (e.g., drinking cup, dagger, stone wrist-guard). In a direct echo of Clarke's ideas, Shennan's view was that this package existed in a social sphere distinct from the rest of the material culture and constituted objects of prestige circulating amongst emerging local élites (Shennan 1976). This emulation network was thus substituted for the idea of the Beaker folk, and the diffusion of practices and ideas took over from the dispersal of individuals as the mechanism of change.

At the same time, several continental scholars were conducting equally groundbreaking research. The Swiss archaeologist Alain Gallay re-considered the Bell Beaker variation through the examination of several distinct facets of the ceramic record, as well as other categories of evidence (e.g., battle axes), and more abstract concepts such as the transition to the Early Bronze Age, leading him to define the phenomenon as a series of networks. In line with the strong formal reasoning which characterised his epistemological work, he eventually identified five diffusion networks, each with a specific spatial structure that encompassed a new material cartography of the Bell Beaker Phenomenon (Gallay 1973).

The 1980s and 1990s are often considered a quieter period in the Bell Beaker historiography, overshadowed by the interpretative monuments laid out by Clarke and Shennan (e.g., Shennan 1986, 1993; see also Brodie 1994, 1997 for an insightful analysis of the many variations of the prestige model). But the year 1987 also saw the publication of an influential paper by Andrew Sherratt revisiting the long-assumed link between bell beakers and alcoholic beverages (Sherratt 1987). Sherratt's argument rests upon the intuition that the production of alcoholic drinks was made more readily possible thanks to the access to new resources, facilitated by Sherratt's own Secondary Products Revolution (Sherratt 1981), and that the consumption of these beverages was embedded in ritual practices performed by social élites. While Sherratt's focus on the production of drinks is arguably innovative, conceptually speaking his eventual scenario does not differ significantly from the one outlined in Childe's aforementioned quote.

By contrast, from the late 1990s onwards, the Bell Beaker historiography was characterised by a growing awareness of the limits of these theoretical models, and in particular their poor fit with the data (e.g., absence of graves meeting the criteria of the canonical definition of the package: Salanova 1998; largely local production of bell beakers, contrary to the predictions of the prestige model: Salanova et al. 2016). As a consequence, scholars all over Europe embarked upon a renewed, though not coordinated, re-evaluation of the material culture. Noticeably, Laure Salanova showed that bell beakers were often decorated using a narrow set of rules and tools (e.g., cardium shell) and suggested that only a comparatively limited number of vessels were typologically coherent enough to constitute a pan-European commonality (so-called 'standard': Salanova 2000). In the footsteps of Alain Gallay, Marie Besse demonstrated the existence of regional traditions in the oft-neglected domestic ceramic assemblages in which the bell beakers appear (e.g., Besse 2003), and comparable results have been obtained for lithics, another historically overlooked category of evidence (e.g., Furestier 2007; Bailly 2014). More synthetic accounts include my own attempt at applying widely Clarke's polythetic notion of culture on a combination of traits (ceramic decoration and morphology, funerary practices, and settlement patterns: Vander Linden 2006), and, more recently, Kleijne's formal application of network theory (Kleijne 2019). The resulting literature is vast, scattered across many papers, monographs, conference proceedings, and edited volumes (e.g., Nicolis 2001, Fokkens and Nicolis 2012; Czebreszuk 2014; Gibson 2019a). Thanks to this vast undertaking, we now possess a much improved empirical data set, without which the present element would simply be impossible. It is also worth pointing out that a coherent descriptive vocabulary and/or standardised terminology are still lacking. Although much of this work grew out of discontent with existing theories, there has been a comparative dearth of new theoretical developments and, despite its many criticisms, the prestige model for instance remains widely quoted in several regional traditions (e.g., Garrido-Pena 1997, 2019). This being said, there is an implicit consensus that no single explanatory factor can account for the entire variation of the Bell Beaker Phenomenon, and that narrowing down its material definition to a few chosen traits has proved a fallacy.

1.3 New Techniques, Old Ideas: The Return of the Beaker Folk

It is a cliché to state that scientific progress is intimately linked to technological advances, and like any other cliché, this one has limited value. While the radiocarbon revolution was instrumental in the way archaeologists have tackled processes such as the spread of early farming or megalithism, its impact upon Bell Beaker studies was minimal. In the same vein, this section is built on a simple idea. Without denying the technical achievements of strontium isotope analysis and ancient DNA, that their recent success in Bell Beaker circles owes an extensive debt to this paradoxical combination of increased empirical knowledge and yet has remained a relative interpretative vacuum.

The first steps towards reconsidering the role of human mobility during this period were provided by the results of Sr analysis for a selection of central European Bell Beaker cemeteries (Price et al. 1998, 2004). These papers demonstrated that a substantial fraction of the buried individuals had relocated between their places of birth and death, although there were no discernible patterns regarding the identity of these 'non-locals' (e.g., sex-based). Despite the pioneering nature of this research, it was a different find that truly sent shockwaves through the discipline. The grave known as the 'Amesbury Archer' was discovered prior to the construction of a housing development in the vicinity of Stonehenge. Not only is the burial exceptional due to the large and outlandish range of associated grave goods (Fitzpatrick 2013; see Section 3) but, more crucially, isotopic analysis indicates that this individual came from continental central Europe. Together with other sites (e.g., 'Boscombe bowmen': Evans et al. 2006), these studies ignited a necessary reconsideration of the importance of mobility, and of the potential underlying social mechanisms of such movement (e.g., post-marital residency rules: Vander Linden 2007) during this period. However, the impact of isotopic analysis remained minimal, largely due to the limits of the technique in pinpointing with certainty the area of origin of 'non-local' individuals (Bentley 2006; Britton et al. 2021). As such, these results cannot be readily interpreted in terms of population history, which would be necessary to postulate an episode of dispersal of individuals of significant scale and magnitude to shape local demographic regimes. It is only over the past decade that such results have become available due to the development of new generation sequencing of ancient DNA.

Spring 2015 saw the publication in close succession of two papers which independently showed that the Corded Ware Complex of central and northern Europe was associated with the introduction of a new ancestry component in the genetic landscape of later prehistoric Europe (Allentoft et al. 2015; Haak et al. 2015).[1] The extensive proportion of this ancestry carried by multiple individuals indicates the robustness of these results: there is no denying that a migration happened in this area at the beginning of the 3rd millennium calBC, although many discussions – healthily so – continue with regard to the exact corresponding social mechanisms and their relationships with the archaeological record (e.g., Furholt 2018, 2019; Kristiansen 2022). The putative link between archaeological material culture and genetic relatedness was at the core of a large-scale aDNA study on the Bell Beaker Phenomenon published in 2018 (Olalde et al. 2018). Based on extensive, though geographically uneven, sampling of individuals, Olalde and collaborators confirmed that the Bell Beaker Phenomenon marks the introduction of this steppe ancestry into other parts of Europe. Yet, in contrast to the initial naive claims of one-on-one identity between the Corded Ware Complex and the proposed 'steppe ancestry', there appears to be more genetic variation in the Bell Beaker samples, pointing to differing scales in this process of human dispersal (Figure 2). The extremes of this range are best encapsulated by, on the one hand, Britain with a – debatable (e.g., Booth et al. 2021) – suggestion of near entire population turnover, and, on the other hand, a limited incidence of 'steppe ancestry' across the Iberian Peninsula (see Sections 3, 4).

This is not the right moment to discuss the pros and cons of ancient DNA. For the time being, to paraphrase the proverbial storm in a teacup, the ripples generated by isotopic and aDNA research are merely proportional to the deceptive *status quaestionis* regarding the interpretation of the Bell Beaker Phenomenon. As seen, thematic consistency pervades Bell Beaker historiography, and such disciplinary dependability is fragile. This is not to say that previous generations lacked any form of imagination but rather that they only engaged in a relatively superficial way with questions of space, time, variation,

---

[1] The geographical origin of this new set of genes is to be sought in the North Pontic Steppe and is thus often referred to as 'steppe ancestry', an implicit convention followed here.

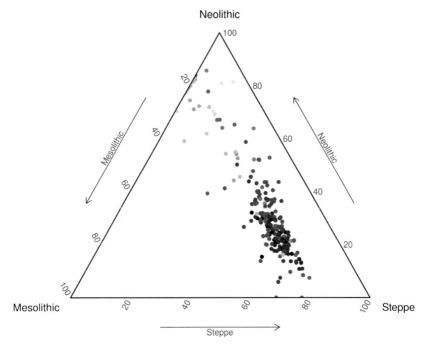

Figure 2 ternary chart of BB ancestry, using foragers, farmers, and Shading indicates latitude (data after Racimo et al. 2020).

and human dispersal, and how these four traits combine to constitute the unique architecture of the Bell Beaker Phenomenon.

1.4 So, What Is This Element All About?

The challenge of this Element is to show how an old concept, archaeological culture, and four long-recognised traits can help us in shaping an analytical framework to, first, account for the vast and unstructured data produced over the past couple of decades and, second, offer a hopefully original take on the period.

The first objective is thus to synthesize, within the bounds of the present editorial format, the Bell Beaker material variation. After discussing chron-ology and geography in Section 2, Section 3 aims at providing a partial, yet representative view of the existing data. This section constitutes the bulk of the text and is organised in loose geographical terms, as such an outline has the advantage of retaining the simple fact that the archaeological record stems from the agency and action of people who lived together, did and practised different things, and possibly drew boundaries between these different spheres of activ-ity. This undertaking is explicitly polythetic as it aims to account for multiple categories of evidence without reifying any of them. In this sense, this Element does not assume the existence of a putative Bell Beaker identity, nor does it aim at providing a material definition of the Bell Beaker culture. Rather, the objective is to characterise the variation of archaeological contexts grouped under that label and, from there, to infer processes responsible for such variation. It is also noteworthy that this presentation does not claim to be exhaustive and thus, from time to time, casts its gaze over several well-rehearsed themes.

The previous pages have shown that any solution to the Bell Beaker problem does not rest solely on the development and application of new techniques but must engage with a robust theoretical framework. To this purpose, my personal inclination lies in ecology and the breadth of concepts and tools it has to offer. Themes of space, variation, and dispersal all strongly resonate with the ecological notion of connectivity, that is, the flow of individuals, matter, and energy within and between habitats, and a key property in explaining their formation and conservation. In this sense, the differences between archaeology and ecology are perhaps not as marked as one may think. Both tackle an equally complex web of networks encompassing movement of individuals, while ecology's interest in matter and energy can be substituted for archaeology's focus on objects and ideas. As explored in Section 4, such an ecological take helps us to re-assess the undeniable qualitative difference that distinguishes the Bell Beaker Phenomenon from the other European prehistoric behemoths and makes it possible to re-evaluate its role in shaping the historical trajectories of the following centuries.

2 Where and When?

2.1 Where and Where Not

Perhaps the most obvious and eye-catching trait of the Bell Beaker Phenomenon is its geographic range. With finds distributed from Ireland in the west to central Hungary in the east, and from Norway to the north all the way to Morocco to the south, the spatial spread of the Bell Beaker Phenomenon is unique in later European prehistory and unchallenged in extent until the expansion of the Roman Empire in the first centuries AD. Beyond its vast geographic footprint, two other fundamental properties set this phenomenon apart from any other European prehistoric complexes.

The first property is best encapsulated by translating the geographical reach of the Bell Beaker Phenomenon into numbers: in longitudinal degrees it spans between c. 10° W and 20° E, or over 2000 km, and in latitudinal degrees, from c. 60° N to 35° N, or over 2500 km (Figure 3). While the longitudinal spread of the Bell Beaker Phenomenon is assuredly impressive, it is actually on par with,

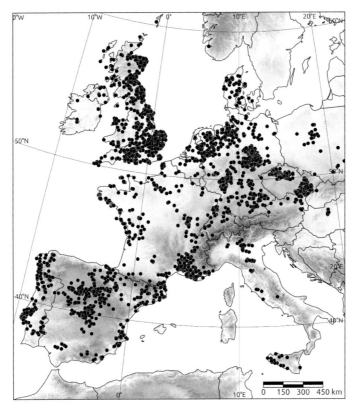

Figure 3 Distribution map of Bell Beaker sites (data after Bilger 2019).

if not less than, that of the other later prehistoric behemoths mentioned earlier. However, for the first time in Holocene European prehistory, we observe here a process with a strongly latitudinal distribution. For instance, the early spread of farming occurs within two latitudinal bands and corresponding ecological niches, loosely associated with distinct archaeological complexes, namely the LBK and Impressa-Cardial (Banks et al. 2013). Despite the contemporary and later circulation of goods (e.g., Pétrequin et al. 2012), practices (e.g., Salavert et al. 2020), and individuals (e.g., Rivollat et al. 2015), interactions between these two bands remained minimal. Likewise, the Corded Ware Complex only occupies a relatively narrow latitudinal band.

Chronologically speaking, the Bell Beaker Phenomenon spans the so-called 4.2 climatic event, which formally marks the transition between the middle and the late Holocene. It is, however, noteworthy that the exact magnitude of this climate event, and its impact upon local environments, remains uncertain, and most likely did not lead to any extensive temperature and/or precipitation shifts across Europe (e.g., Bini et al. 2019; Bradley and Bakke 2019). Therefore,

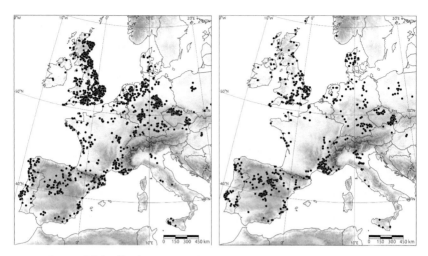

Figure 4 Distribution maps of Bell Beaker funerary sites (left) and settlements (right) (data after Bilger 2019).

although the precise bounds of biogeographical and climatic divisions remain difficult to pinpoint with great precision for this period, one can consider that their modern distribution provides a robust analogue. This minor clarification matters in the sense that the Bell Beaker local groups encompass a diversity of regional landscapes, biomes, and climatic zones.

Because of the general paucity of settlements across much of the domain (Figure 4; see Section 3), it is difficult to assess with absolute certainty how much this ecological diversity is mirrored by a variety of food acquisition strategies and settlement patterns, although most of the evidence suggests that it does, a point addressed in the next chapter. Regardless, the implications of the environmental variability are essential. Assuming that some level of connectivity links together these local groups, whatever the exact factors at play are, it seems unlikely that they are to be sought in the realms of subsistence. Most fundamentally, it is noteworthy that Bell Beaker connectivity bridged ecological divides which had so far played a structuring role in the cultural geography of Holocene Europe.

The second property of the Bell Beaker Phenomenon has long been recognised. The numbers quoted above suggest a territory covering four to five million square kilometres. Yet, a quick glance at the maps (Figures 3–4) demonstrates how misleading this figure is, as we are not dealing with a continuous distribution but rather a patchwork of spatially disconnected groups. The tension between fragmented and unified cartographies of the Bell Beaker Phenomenon is long-lasting and underscores two diverging views of the period, one explicitly tackling variation, and one leaning towards the identification of commonalities across the domain. Mapping this phenomenon accurately has proved an arduous task given its presence in multiple countries and traditions of research, but also, most importantly, because of the lack of any

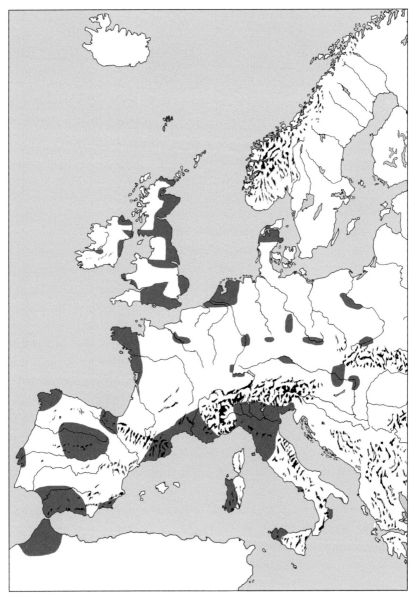

Figure 5 Geographical extent of regional Bell Beaker groups
as per 2006 (after Vander Linden 2006).

agreed, overarching, material definitions. Figure 5 offers a picture of the state of affairs at the beginning of the 2000s. Twenty years later, it ought to be possible to assess its accuracy, and, yet at the time of writing, there is still no Bell Beaker atlas in the sense of a comprehensive georeferenced dataset of archaeological sites and finds. There are, however, a few regional maps and site gazetteers (e.g., Nicolis 2001; Fokkens et al. 2016; Lemercier et al. 2019). At a larger scale, the only attempt at a site-based cartography is that published by Michael Bilger (2019), which forms the empirical basis of Figure 3. Although his synthesis does not claim to be exhaustive, it presents a transparent methodology as its maps are built from the compilation of site-based information, rather than inferring local distributions from the literature. As Bilger himself acknowledges (Bilger, personal communication Oct. 2022), the result is far from complete and therefore ought to be used with caution and is unfit for statistical purposes. Yet, it offers a rare snapshot of the Bell Beaker cartography.

At first sight, this map confirms the discontinuous character of the distribution. Or, put more simply, this map stands out for both the extent of Bell Beaker regional groups and for the lack of them. However, this impression should not be taken at face-value as the problem lies in evaluating the nature of empty spaces and the density of the existing groups. The latter is hardly informative, especially in light of the aforementioned limits of Bilger's data collection, and also because it is notably difficult to assess site density without any in-depth knowledge of local archaeological practices (e.g., areas that might be over-represented due to the intensity of development-led fieldwork). Visual comparison with published regional maps suggests a general level of accuracy, though certain areas with known Bell Beaker sites are under-represented (e.g., southeastern France: Lemercier et al. 2019) if not absent (e.g., Sardinia: Melis 2019).

As noted above, this distribution is noticeable for its alternation of filled and void areas. The Iberian Peninsula presents a strong Atlantic representation from Galicia to the Tagus estuary, but not in the southernmost tip, occupied by the contemporary Ferradeira horizon (Valera et al. 2019). Further inland, a large central group stretches from the Basque country to the Meseta. There, the Bell Beaker presence is clearly documented, though in several instances, it is rather diffuse within existing cultural traditions so that local specialists speak of sites with Bell Beakers rather than Bell Beaker sites (Garrido-Pena 2019; see Section 3). The same distinction applies to Mediterranean France, where, alongside contemporary Late Neolithic groups, sites yield assemblages with varying degrees of Bell Beaker material culture (Lemercier et al. 2019). The rest of the Western Mediterranean basin is characterised by a comparable mix of areas rich in Bell Beaker finds, and areas devoid of them but occupied by other archaeological groups, such as along the eastern coast of Iberia, the Italian

Tyrrhenian coast, or in Sicily. Further north, the Saône-Rhône axis plays a structuring role as a north–south corridor, contrasting with the discontinuous distribution of Atlantic France, with empty areas such as the Landes, seemingly an ecological wasteland for much of later prehistory. Few but significant Bell Beaker finds are known in Normandy (e.g., Marcigny et al. 2003, 2004) and along the Seine River, but in lesser quantity in northern France and in the Paris basin, where they coincide with sites with other types of material assemblages (Salanova et al. 2011). Ecology is arguably the biggest factor in shaping settlement pattern in the Netherlands, which was dominated by large areas of peatland unsuitable for human settlement (Fokkens et al. 2016). Bell Beaker groups extend further in northern Germany, but then abruptly stop before resuming in northern Jutland. The position of the latter is largely dictated by its late chronology (see below), and once more the apparent gaps are actually filled by sites with non-Beaker material culture (Sarauw 2019). Not featuring on this map, a few Bell Beaker finds are present in coastal Norway (Prescott 2020). To the east, there are clear concentrations along the Rhine and Danube river valleys, as well as in Bohemia, Moravia, and Poland (Turek 2019). The easternmost Bell Beaker group is located in central Hungary, alongside several local Early Bronze Age groups (Reményi et al. 2019). Lastly, the distribution in Britain presents a strong bias towards the eastern coast, and Bell Beaker finds in Ireland remain sporadic within an otherwise rich archaeological landscape (Carlin 2018; Gibson 2019b).

Although the state of documentation has improved and fieldwork has filled in a few gaps over the past two decades, the picture remains one of spatially disconnected groups whose separation is structured by a complex mix of landscape affordances and areas with other contemporaneous archaeological expressions, and whose connection seems to favour corridors provided by major river valleys and maritime littorals.

2.2 Time matters, or the never-ending quest for a homeland

The geographic fragmentation of the Bell Beaker Phenomenon is reinforced by its chronology since several of these groups are either not contemporaneous or characterised by divergent typological and historical trajectories. However, the current state of the radiocarbon documentation does not allow us to validate this point systematically in a quantitative way. Unlike other prehistoric processes, there is no comprehensive gazetteer of radiocarbon dates for the entire Bell Beaker Phenomenon apart from a few high-quality regional datasets (e.g., Beckerman 2011–12; Parker Pearson et al. 2019). Even though several inclusive repositories have thousands of dates for the period under consideration, it is often impossible to connect these data with high-resolution contextual informa-tion, especially typological attribution of the corresponding archaeological contexts.

It is tempting to view this state of affairs as an unfortunate consequence of a limited lack of engagement with radiocarbon and associated quantitative modelling within Bell Beaker academic circles. As we have seen, the publica-tion of the Dutch Model in the mid-1970s triggered a passion for placing the mythical homeland in the Netherlands, rather than a methodological interest in replicating these results and techniques. Although regional programmes were undertaken (e.g., Britain: Kinnes et al. 1991), the quantity of data available today stems more from the increased application of radiocarbon dating within the discipline more generally than from targeted dating programmes. Likewise, while existing reviews all point to the existence of early dates in the Iberian Peninsula (e.g., Müller and van Willingen 2001), none of them attempt to apply any of the quantitative methods that could help in identifying a spatio-temporal structure potentially informative of a dispersal process, as has been carried out for the spread of early farming for instance.

In all fairness, such methodological sophistication would be hindered by the tortuous shape of the radiocarbon calibration curve for the 3rd millennium calBC, which is marked by a flat-ish section between c. 2800 and 2600 calBC, followed by a couple of steep wiggles until c. 2475 calBC, and another flat segment until c. 2200calBC (Reimer et al. 2020; Figure 6). Despite many technical and methodological improvements in the technique (e.g., more accur-ate calibration curves, gradual lowering of the standard deviation for new dates, and application of Bayesian statistics for regional or site sequences), the ups and downs of the curve remain an obstacle which needs to be factored into any assessment of the Bell Beaker chronology. Keeping this in mind together with the state of the evidence, the following investigative approaches attempt to evaluate the interplay between the geography and temporality of the Bell Beaker Phenomenon, and how in concert they constitute a key component of any analytical assessment of its variation.

Even prior to the days of radiocarbon dating, the Iberian Peninsula, and especially the Portuguese Estremadura, has been in the running as one of the main contenders for the coveted status of Bell Beaker homeland. And indeed, only this area yields numerous dates falling between c. 2700 and 2450 calBC. Although these dates come from several sites (e.g., Leceia, Porto das Carretas, Miguens 3, Perdigões: Cardoso 2014; Valera et al. 2019), stratigraphic and typological issues preclude any Bayesian modelling (e.g., problems of residuality and contamination for the Zambujal sequence: Kleijne 2019). Typological uncer-tainty also mars the credentials of the area as a homeland candidate, as there is

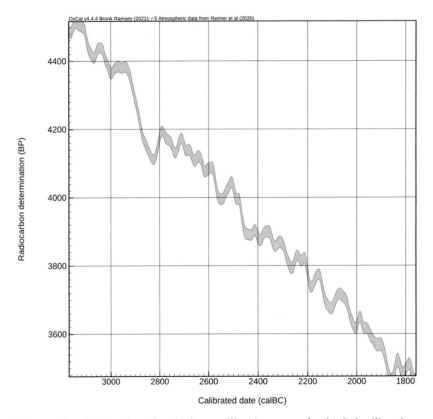

Figure 6 Intcal20 northern hemisphere calibration curve for the 3rd millennium calBC (after Reimer et al. 2020).

a limited consensus on whether local ceramic productions can be regarded as prototypes for Bell Beaker pottery or not (Cardoso 2014). Stylistically speaking, so-called Maritime beakers appear throughout the 3rd millennium calBC across the entire Iberian Peninsula, sometimes alongside regional styles (e.g., de Jesus Sanches and Barbosa 2018). From c. 2400–2300 calBC onwards, local sequences are characterised by increased regionalisation, eventually leading to the development of local facies, such as the Ciempozuelos group.

Another local sequence with a long pedigree in the competition for the title of Bell Beaker homeland is the Netherlands. Originally based solely on typological grounds, the Dutch model has gone through numerous versions over several decades, and its many iterations have all placed data hygiene at the forefront through rigorous assessment of sample quality (e.g., old wood effect, link between date and ceramic type). Beckerman's recent appraisal considers that almost 50per cent of available dates have to be rejected on such grounds (Beckerman 2011–2). On this basis and through visual inspection of the date

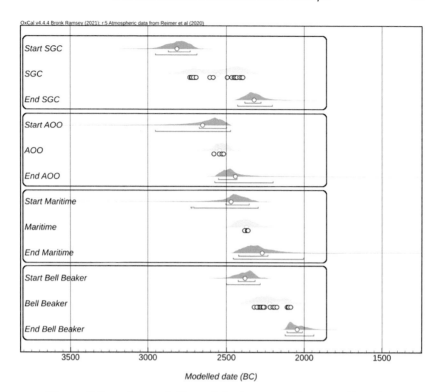

Figure 7 Bayesian modelling of single grave culture – Bell Beaker Phenomenon typo-chronological development in the Netherlands (data after Beckerman 2011–2; created using Oxcal v4.4 and Intcal20: Bronk Ramsey 2017; Reimer et al. 2020).

probabilities, she concludes that it is impossible to test the validity of the specific typological schemes posed by many authors (e.g., Single Grave Culture (SGC) – All-Over-Ornamented (AOO) beakers – Maritime beakers), although the continuity between the Single Grave Complex and the Bell Beaker (BB) Phenomenon is undeniable. Figure 7 provides a Bayesian model of Beckerman's data, by considering the SGC, AOO, Maritime, and other BB ceramic productions as overlapping phases. Despite issues linked to the limited number of dates and the shape of the curve, its results confirm Beckerman's conclusion, with the SGC and AOO styles presented as strictly contemporaneous and dated to the first half of the 3rd millennium calBC, followed by the Maritime and Bell Beaker productions, which largely overlap during the second half of the same millennium. From this perspective, while Dutch Maritime bell beakers are thus later than their Iberian counterparts, the overall typological continuity cannot be denied. It is fair to say that, rather than leaving us in the dark as to the question of a homeland, such results demonstrate the limits of typological thinking, and of anchoring the roots of the Bell Beaker Phenomenon in a single, spatially confined area.

In all other regions, radiocarbon dating points to local Bell Beaker sequences starting no earlier than c. 2500calBC, a date strongly correlated to the end of the aforementioned steep wiggle in the radiocarbon curve. Another commonality is the existence of a relatively short first horizon characterised by lower typological variation. In the Paris basin, this first phase is associated with maritime and All-Over-Corded beakers between 2550 and 2450 calBC. It is then followed by two other phases lasting until the beginning of the 2nd millennium calBC (Salanova et al. 2011). Bayesian modelling of the few existing 14 C dates as two overlapping phases, however, indicates that these brackets must be considered with some caution (Figure 8). In a similar vein, Lemercier (2012) has put forward a threefold chronological division of the Bell Beaker sequence in southern France, with a first short phase (2550/2500 to 2400/2350 calBC) marked by relative homogeneity of the ceramic decoration (Maritime, AOC, mixed styles), quickly followed by a second phase which sees the development of multiple regional groups (c. 2400/2350 to 2150calBC). This eventually leads to the transition to the Early Bronze Age. Likewise, in central Europe, Bayesian modelling places the start of the Bell Beaker Phase around 2450calBC, lasting until 2150–2045 calBC (Brunner et al. 2020).

The British sequence rests upon a robust combination of extensive 14 C sampling and Bayesian modelling (Parker Pearson et al. 2019). As elsewhere,

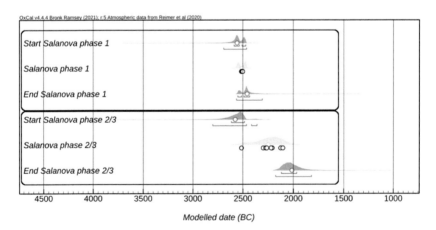

Figure 8 Bayesian modelling of the suggested three-fold chronological development in the Paris Basin (data after Salanova et al. 2011; created using Oxcal v4.4 and Intcal20: Bronk Ramsey 2017; Reimer et al. 2020).

the earliest phase, lasting between 2450/2400 and 2300 calBC, is characterised by a low stylistic ceramic diversity (low-carinated beakers). The picture changes from 2300/2250calBC, with an increased regional variation, especially in funerary contexts, leading to a preferred terminology of 'beakers' in opposition to the rest of the European Bell Beaker traditions. This diversification phase is generally referred to as the 'fission horizon', following Stuart Needham, who first identified this pattern (Needham 2005). Beaker traits last until the early 2nd millennium BC, when they are succeeded by the local Early Bronze Age facies. It is noteworthy that the start of the fission horizon closely matches the beginning of the Bell Beaker presence in Denmark, estimated between 2350/2300 and 1900 calBC (Sarauw 2007).

Although hardly exhaustive, several conclusions can be drawn from this appraisal of the Bell Beaker chronologies. Firstly, the start of the phenomenon lies in the interval between 2700/2600calBC and 2450calBC. At this time, the Portuguese Estremadura is the only area which yields bell beakers in their narrowest typological definition (i.e., maritime style), while the Dutch sequence, for this time bracket, comprises All-Over-Ornamented beakers. Not only is it thus impossible to identify a single putative point of origin from which the Bell Beaker Phenomenon would stem but such reasoning is anyway of limited interest in view of the extensive material variation exhibited by all regional groups (see Section 3). Secondly, there is a wider generalisation of Bell Beaker groups across most of Europe from c.2500/2450 calBC onwards, a process often materialised locally by a limited ceramic typological diversity. Thirdly, from c. 2300 calBC onwards, there seems to be an increased level of regionalisation in pottery styles, which also marks the onset of new regional groups such as in Denmark. From then onwards, the situation becomes blurred, with the inception of the Early Bronze Age varying locally. This means that dependent upon regional typological considerations, terminologies, and research traditions, some of the corresponding groups can either be considered as late Bell Beaker or individualised as Early Bronze Age. In any case, Bell Beaker traits do not seem to extend way beyond 1900calBC.

Altogether, the Bell Beaker Phenomenon can be described as a suite of spatially distinct patches, covering a wide array of potential habitats, and connected for a few centuries by an apparent homogeneity that was gradually encroached on by regionalisation. Admittedly, this description is predicated on the coupling of radiocarbon and pottery typology, but, as the next section demonstrates, it encompasses some of the essential properties of the Bell Beaker Phenomenon.

3 Variation, Variation, Variation

The previous pages led us to conclude that, in spatial terms, the Bell Beaker Phenomenon is best described as a discontinuous patchwork. Although one could theoretically follow this point to its logical conclusion by adopting an atomic stance where each patch is considered in succession, the premise of the entire historiography and of this Element is that some level of connectivity underlies the entire complex. Even the most zealous deniers of archaeological cultures would admit that the mere existence of shared traits is informative about some sort of interaction and/or contacts between past people. The question is what type of interaction, and the answer lies first and foremost in a thorough description of the variation exhibited by the archaeological assemblages involved. This section aims to do that, though the following survey is unapologetically impressionistic and subjective. After a brief assessment of the historical context within which regional sequences unfold, these pages are primarily concerned with linking variation and connectivity, and thus focus on certain categories of evidence: funerary practices, because they generally form the bulk of the documentation; settlement patterns, a trickier source of information but privileged here because they reflect habitat diversity; material culture mostly through the prism of exchange and technological transfer; and lastly, strontium and ancient DNA data as our main proxy for human dispersal.

3.1 Iberian Peninsula

Although radiocarbon dating does not provide a straightforward sequential ordering of the individual Bell Beaker patches, it makes sense to begin with the Portuguese Estremadura and the Iberian Peninsula. Bell Beakers emerge at the end of a long episode of sustained demographic rise beginning in the mid-4th millennium calBC, as suggested by summed probability distributions of radiocarbon dates (hereafter SPDs; Lillios et al. 2016; Blanco-González et al. 2018; Figure 9). This trend is noticeable across the southern half of the peninsula, where the archaeological record has revealed a multiplication of sites, increased diversity, and a marked trend towards monumentality. Firstly, well-rooted in traditions stretching back to the late 5th mill. calBC, megalithism continues to flourish. Necropolises including a wide range of collective burials and architectural forms, some of them with exquisite sophistication, are founded and remain in use during the 3rd millennium calBC (e.g., Valencina de la Concepción: García Sanjuán et al. 2018). Secondly, impressive stone-dry monumental complexes are built, including Leceia, Zambujal, and Los Millares. A more recent addition to the archaeology of the area is the discovery of ditched enclosures. These monumental sites are composed of several concentric ditches up to 400 m in diameter and include

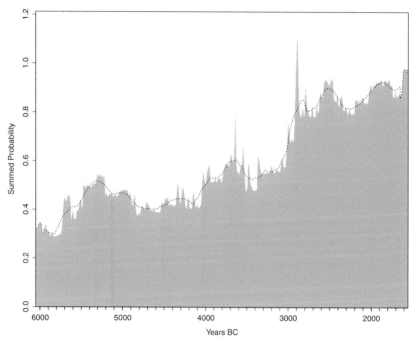

Figure 9 Summed probability distribution of 14 C dates for the Iberian
Peninsula. Dashed lines indicate a running mean of 200 years
(data after Sweeney et al. 2022).

a variety of burials and other deposition practices (e.g., Perdigões, Marroquíes:
Lillios 2020). Both ditched and walled enclosed sites witness human and animal
mobility, though there are no patterns in the proportion of outliers or their spatial
range (e.g., Waterman et al. 2014; Wright et al. 2019; Valera et al. 2020).
The movement of people and animals echoes the vibrant economic life occurring
on these sites, reflected in copper metallurgy and trade (e.g., Murillo-Barroso
et al. 2017), amber sourced from Sicily (Murillo-Barroso et al. 2018), and ivory
from both African savannah and Indian elephants (Schuhmacher et al. 2009;
Nocete et al. 2013).

This combination of traits is often interpreted in terms of emergent social
complexity and stratification (e.g.; Lillios 2020), from which the regional Bell
Beaker Phenomenon would emerge. Several elements indeed point to continuity across the 3rd millennium calBC. More tentatively, the suggestion that
the Bell Beaker Phenomenon stems from a world pervaded by social complexity and competition fits with processual readings cast in terms of élites and
social prestige. A first argument in support of such a thesis would be based on
the discovery of early bell beakers on monumental fortified sites such as in

Leceia and Zambujal in Portugal. In both cases, however, most of the beaker remains were found in peripheral positions in contrast to their presence in other fortified sites built during the late 3rd millennium calBC (Cardoso 2014). Further south in the Alentejo region, Bell Beaker remains are also found on sites displaying evidence for long-term use, such as in Perdigões, where they are associated with the construction of small circular stone structures with radial walls (Valera et al. 2019). On the same site, Bell Beaker pottery was found in association with cremated human remains, and, in another tomb, gold foil ornaments (Monge Soares et al. 2012). Otherwise, the Bell Beaker Phenomenon is generally rare in funerary contexts across the Alentejo, unlike Estremadura, where Bell Beaker material culture is routinely discovered in megalithic monuments, as well as in long-used funerary caves (e.g., Lillios et al. 2010; Zilhão et al. 2022).

This diversity in domestic and funerary sites provides a template for the entire Iberian Peninsula. Galicia hosts Bell Beaker reuse of both older megalithic and previously abandoned Chalcolithic fortified sites, as well as newly created unenclosed settlements (Prieto-Martinez 2019). Across the Meseta, the majority of sites correspond to surface finds, with few associated structures, often located on ridges overlooking rivers and/or terraces, but rarely in caves and/or rock-shelters (Garrido-Pena 2019). In most instances it is notable that pits with Bell Beaker materials are in the minority, suggesting that these are best considered as settlements with bell beakers, rather than Bell Beaker settlements (Garrido-Pena 2019). There are few exceptions to this pattern, and the site of El Ventorro, published in 1992, remains unmatched with its twenty-three pits, two huts, and traces of copper smelting (Priego & Querro 1992). As elsewhere in the Iberian Peninsula and contemporary non-Bell Beaker areas (e.g., Valera et al. 2019; Aranda Jiménez, et al. 2022), the funerary record in the Meseta features a combination of reused megalithic dolmens and caves alongside funerary pits, and the practice of both collective and individual burials (Bueno Ramírez et al. 2005; see also Fernández-Crespo et al. 2019). In addition to bell beakers and numerous other ceramic types, grave good assemblages include several types of ornament (e.g., V-perforated buttons), weapons (e.g., copper daggers, stone wristguards, or slender copper points known as Palmela points, e.g., Soriano et al. 2021), and miniature vessels probably made on purpose for children (Herrero-Corral et al. 2019). One particular site deserves some attention. Humanejos, a cemetery in use from the Chalcolithic to the Bronze Age, includes nine Bell Beaker graves. Tomb 1, a carefully built stone chamber, contained the successive burials of a woman and a man, the latter associated with multiple pots, ornaments (including some made of ivory), a stone bracer, Palmela points, and, exceptionally for Iberia, a halberd (Garrido-Pena et al. 2022; Figure 10).

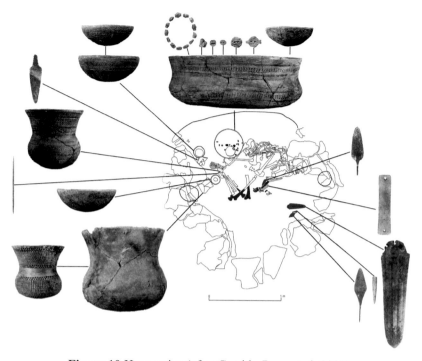

Figure 10 Humanejos (after Garrido-Pena et al. 2022).

The lavishness and repetitive deposition of otherwise equivalent artefacts (e.g., multiple weapons) puts this burial into the category of so-called over-provisioned graves, a particular type which we will encounter on other occasions across the Bell Beaker domain.

Much has been written about the idea that bell beakers were vessels for consuming alcoholic beverages. Yet, empirical confirmation of this putative function is elusive and the literature points to several instances of beakers containing other things than drinks (Brodie 1994). A rare positive identification of drink comes from the site of La Sima, where residue analysis confirmed the presence of a beer-like beverage through identification of cereals, yeast, starch granules showing surface alterations related to germination, and *Calcius oxalate*, a crystalline deposit linked to malt and beer preparation (Rojo-Guerra et al. 2006). Other scientific analyses of pottery have also been undertaken on a relatively large scale over the past few decades in order to test the hypothesis of direct exchange of pottery between communities. Chemical characterization of clay and temper indicates that most vessels were produced with locally available raw materials; for example, in Galicia, a third of the pots were made from clay sourced from within a 7-km radius, and the rest from a maximum distance of 37 km (Salanova et al. 2016). This pattern, repeated in other regions, contrasts with long-distance technological similarities between Galicia and Brittany, indicated by the use of kaolin for white incrustation, and of the use of donax and cockle shells for impressed decoration (Prieto-Martinez & Salanova 2009). In Alentejo, the presence of only a few pottery imports suggests that bell beakers were added to the local ceramic repertoire (Dias et al. 2017). Other categories of evidence point to continuing economic dynamism: copper metallurgy, including production workshops (e.g., Dorado Alejos et al. 2021; Montes-Landa et al. 2021), and acquisition of amber with multiple origins, including locally and from Sicily (Murillo-Barroso et al. 2018).

As is always the case in Bell Beaker studies, the question of the movement of goods leads to a discussion regarding the scale and nature of human mobility. Strontium isotope analyses indicate a variety of scenarios (e.g., Waterman et al. 2014; Díaz-del-Río et al. 2022), often with a low level of mobility but sometimes with indications of movement over longer distance and involving more individuals, as is the case at the early 2nd millennium calBC site of Valdescusa (Ortega et al. 2021). It is noteworthy that this diversity is echoed by work undertaken on contemporaneous non–Bell Beaker sites (Díaz-Zorita Bonilla et al. 2018). Ancient DNA provides a different view of mobility. The second half of the 3rd millennium calBC, and thus the Bell Beaker Phenomenon, marks the introduction in Iberia of the steppe ancestry genetic signature, though at a much lower level than elsewhere (Olalde et al. 2018). This genomic component reaches a higher proportion in the succeeding Early Bronze Age, including in areas lying outside of the Bell Beaker range (e.g., El Argar culture in south-eastern Spain: Olalde et al. 2019; Villalba-Mouco et al. 2021). This intriguing result suggests that the connections established during the Bell Beaker period remained active for several centuries and eventually spilled over spatially. Lastly, one must also point out the existence of a few individuals throughout the 3rd millennium calBC who show signs of North African ancestry (González-Fortes et al. 2019; Olalde et al. 2019). This last find echoes the discovery of various goods sourced from northern Africa, and the presence of numerous Bell Beakers in the coastal and hinterland Maghreb (e.g., Nekkal and Mikdad 2014).

All in all, one is left with a strong sense of continuity across time and space, as the Bell Beaker Phenomenon appears firmly embedded in the dynamics of the earlier phases of the Chalcolithic, and in the wider variation of contemporaneous Iberian communities. A certain sense of incipient social complexity is inescapable, though perhaps taking different forms in the late 3rd millennium calBC. The Bell Beaker Phenomenon across the Iberian Peninsula thus is marked by a new material culture added to an existing set of social and cultural practices, rather than a radical upheaval. Ancient DNA results similarly point to the inception of the new steppe ancestry in the local genomic landscape instead of a massive population turnover. Yet, it would be too hasty, especially at this stage of the inquiry, to draw any parallel between material culture and genetics.

3.2 Another Homeland? The Low Countries

Let us contrast Iberia with the lower Rhine basin, the other area often quoted as a potential Bell Beaker homeland. As discussed previously, the cultural background here corresponds to the Single Grave Culture, which constitutes the western-most facet of the Corded Ware Complex. Due to the quasi-general absence of bone samples caused by soil acidity, the assimilation of this complex with an episode of mass migration in this region has to be assessed using more traditional categories of archaeological evidence, thus allowing Dutch scholars to investigate these historical trajectories at multiple scales. While older megalithic tombs are reused, the main innovation of the period is the appearance across the landscape of circular funerary barrows, generally covering one or several individual burials, a practice recorded across the entire Corded Ware distribution (Bourgeois 2013). Links with the rest of the complex are also visible in the way bodies are placed on a roughly east–west axis, either in a left (for women) or right (for men) crouched position facing south. Grave good choices echo wider Corded Ware trends, with ceramic offerings dominated by beakers and amphorae, various types of ornaments, and so-called battle axes. Often interpreted in a context of interpersonal violence, recent traceo-logical analysis suggests that these were utilitarian tools linked to deforestation (Wentink 2020). Large-scale network analysis of body and grave good position further demonstrates how funerary Single Grave Culture preferences were part of a widely shared set of rules, characterised by higher formality (i.e., reduced variation) for men's burials (Bourgeois & Kroon 2017). Pottery techniques suggest that the introduction of the Single Grave Culture in the coastal Netherlands took the form of more of a patchwork process, with both imports and traces of technological continuity (Kroon et al. 2019).

Pottery plays a fundamental role in the idea of an unbroken local development from the Single Grave Culture to the Bell Beaker Phenomenon. The hypothesis of a continuous tradition bridging both complexes in the Netherlands is generally accepted, with debates focusing on the precise shape of this typological transition. A narrative of continuity is supported by other categories of evidence. In contrast with most Bell Beaker regions, settlement patterns are well documented for the Netherlands, largely owing to intensive development-led fieldwork and subsequent synthesis (Fokkens et al. 2016). The area stands out because of the nature of the Holocene landscape, with its diversity of marsh ridges, floodplains, fens, peatland, and changing coastlines (Figure 11). Late Neolithic human communities took full

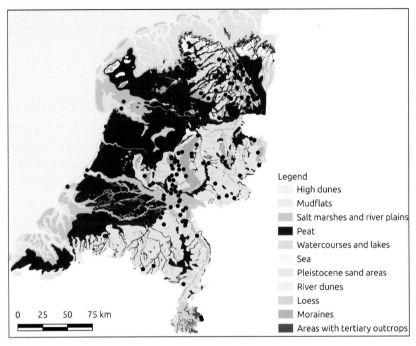

Legend
　　High dunes
　　Mudflats
　　Salt marshes and river plains
　　Peat
　　Watercourses and lakes
　　Sea
　　Pleistocene sand areas
　　River dunes
　　Loess
　　Moraines
　　Areas with tertiary outcrops

0   25   50   75 km

Figure 11 Distribution map of recently identified Dutch Bell Beaker sites against palaeoecological zones (background map, www.cultureelerfgoed.nl/onderwerpen/bronnen-en-kaarten/documenten/publicaties/2019/01/01/paleogeografische-kaarten-zip; data after Bilger 2019, with addition from Bradley et al. 2016).

advantage of the resulting multiplicity of available eco-zones by making use of an extended farming system in which agriculture and herding were supplemented by fishing, hunting, and gathering (Fokkens et al. 2016). There is, however, more uncertainty regarding the nature of building plans. Fokkens and colleagues consider that the Dutch territory has not yielded any convincing house plans for the Bell Beaker period and the Early Bronze Age (Fokkens et al. 2016). This position can be contrasted with the views of Kleijne and Drenth (2019), who mention some – questionable in my opinion – reconstructions, especially for the very late 3rd–early 2nd millennium calBC (e.g., Molenaarsgraf, Noordwijck-Bronsgeest). Nevertheless, the development of a two-aisled building tradition during the Late Neolithic and Early Bronze Age is not in doubt.

A recurrent trait of the Late Neolithic in the Low Countries is a landscape dotted by barrows. Here again, the Bell Beaker Phenomenon exhibits continuity with the Single Grave tradition while also significantly departing from it, with barrows often built a few hundreds of metres apart and rarely in groups of more than three monuments (Bougeois 2013). The same general impression of continuity holds for other facets of the funerary record. Ceramics, and especially beakers, retain their privileged status as grave goods, as do weapons, although archery items (stone bracers, arrowheads), and daggers are substituted for battle-axes (Wentink 2020). The occurrence of cushion-stones and hammers at Hengelo and other sites testifies to the practice of copper metallurgy and the recognised status of the craftworkers (Drenth et al. 2016). There is much variation in the placement of the dead in the grave, and no clear shift in the main axis from the preceding period, unlike central Europe during this period. The picture is, however, blurred by the generally poor preservation of skeletal remains. In this context, the exceptional Niersen burial is worth highlighting (Bourgeois et al. 2009). This barrow was excavated in 1907 and led to the discovery of a burial with human remains. Given the rarity of such finds in a Dutch context, the foresighted decision was made to lift and preserve the burial in its entirety. Recent re-examination of the archives and the remains indicates an open wooden chamber comprising two individuals, the first to be deposited represented by disarticulated remains and the second in an articulated position. Unfortunately, due to the state of the documentation, it is impossible to evaluate with precision the timing of this succession (i.e., either whether both bodies were deposited placed in a single event or the remains of the first individual were pushed to the side when the second individual was interred).

The acidity of the sandy soils also limits the application of any form of laboratory analysis, either strontium isotopes or ancient DNA. Isotope studies are simply non-existent for Late Neolithic human remains, while aDNA analysis is confined to a handful of individuals from a single site (Olalde et al. 2018). This point is far from anecdotal, as these samples provide a key data point in the identification of a massive population turnover in Britain, a contentious point to which we will return later. Since further samples have become available from the sites of Ottoland and Molenaarsgraf, all results point to these individuals deriving c. 60 per cent of their ancestry from the steppe (Patterson et al. 2021).

As for Iberia, multiple lines of evidence converge towards an impression of cultural continuity across the 3rd millennium calBC in the Lower Rhine area. Some changes are noticeable, for instance in the funerary realms, and point to amendments to rules set within the general framework established during the Single Grave period. But the Iberian–Dutch parallel stops there, and both sequences unfold within markedly distinct social ambiances and cultural backgrounds.

3.3 Atlantic Europe

Between these two potential homelands lies a vibrant cultural space stretching from the Bay of Biscay to the shores of the Channel. During the late 4th and early 3rd millennium calBC the Atlantic continental façade witnessed various interaction processes. Perhaps the most well-known of these corresponds to the diffusion of Grand-Pressigny flint daggers. Although there is a large degree of variation in this raw material, it is distinctive; this honey-coloured flint was extracted and knapped into long daggers, and a few other tool types, in various workshops in the Touraine region of central France. From there, daggers were distributed during the late 4th and the early 3rd millennium BC across large areas, with a noticeable concentration along the Atlantic coast and in particular the Morbihan, pointing to a well-established maritime trade network (Ihuel 2014). Grand-Pressigny daggers are under-represented in the rest of Brittany, and in nearby Normandy, but are found in northern France and Belgium, with the northernmost examples occurring in AOO burials in the Netherlands. Another continental Atlantic network can be inferred from the discovery of large rectangular buildings from the Dordogne to northern France and Belgian Flanders. This loose architectural tradition encompasses large-scale to fully monumental buildings, generally found in isolation or in small groups of two to four. In several instances, such as in Brittany and Hauts-de-France, clusters of sites with shared architectural traits point to well-established micro-regional communities of practice (Joseph et al. 2011; Tinévez 2022). These sites, often enclosed, encompass a wide variety of functions and activities, with settlements involved in specific tasks such as linen processing in northern France for instance (Martial et al. 2013). Despite undeniable variety, it is hard to eschew the view that these various local areas are all connected within a relatively coherent cultural koinè. In parallel with this apparent homogeneity, Late Neolithic communities along the Atlantic façade also present marked idiosyncrasies as demonstrated in funerary practices and ceramic typology.

This intricate mix of local and pan-regional expressions extends further during the Bell Beaker period. Variation is evident in the funerary sphere, with several areas containing few individual graves (Salanova 2011), but there are hotspots of collective burials and reuse of megalithic architecture, as in Brittany (Favrel & Nicolas 2022). A closer look at some of the individual graves reveals an intriguing pattern: a couple of graves found at Ciry-Salsogne and Jablines, in the Paris Basin rather than along the Atlantic coast stricto sensu, have both yielded AOC beakers associated with Grand-Pressigny flint daggers, funerary packages strongly reminiscent of Dutch examples though both graves postdate by a century or two the corresponding typological phase in the Netherlands (Salanova 2011). Noticeably, the individual buried at Ciry-Salsogne presents high level of steppe ancestry (Brunel et al. 2020). Likewise, though further south and at a later date (c. 2350–2200 calBC), the grave of Poitiers – La Folie included an AOO beaker and was surrounded by an incomplete circular ring of posts, which would appear alien in the Low Countries (Tchéréminisoff et al. 2011). To this brief set of northerly influenced graves, one can add the old discovery of Wallers – Arenberg in northern France with two beakers with strong Dutch or British Late Beaker typological connections, a chronological attribution which cannot be tested in the absence of bones suitable for radiocarbon (Salanova et al. 2011). Finally, let us mention several individual graves from Normandy, sometimes associated with settlements and dated to the latest centuries of the 3rd millennium BC and thus attributed to the Early Bronze rather than the Bell Beaker Phenomenon per se (Marcigny & Ghesquière 2003; Marcigny et al. 2004; Billard 2011).

Bell Beaker material culture is also routinely found in collective burials and megalithic monuments, though in most cases the long and complex history of use and reuse of these sites precludes precise evaluation of the Bell Beaker context (Favrel & Nicolas 2022). An exception is provided by the chance discovery of the Tumulus des Sables in Aquitaine (James et al. 2019). This non-megalithic collective burial comprised the remains of around thirty individuals, with radiocarbon dating indicating a first use in the Middle Neolithic, and a main period of human deposition during the Bell Beaker period. Sr and O isotope analyses point to very limited human mobility, with a single individual identified as non-local. Otherwise, the main concentration of Bell Beaker finds in megalithic tombs lies in southern Brittany, with a plethora of beakers and arrowheads (Nicolas 2017). These squared barbed and tanged arrowheads are generally made of non-local raw material, and technological analysis points to limited required skills, and thus to individually, rather than specialised, crafted products. Noticeably, these are sometimes encountered in vast quantities at a single site, with a maximum example of sixty, echoing the previously encountered notion of funerary over-provisioning. It is also noteworthy that this particular type has a long-standing pedigree in Atlantic France, starting in the local Late Neolithic, and with Bell Beaker-influenced types being a common occurrence in Early Bronze Age barrows, the latter process is also observed in Britain and Denmark (Nicolas 2017).

In comparison to the Late Neolithic rectangular buildings, continental Atlantic Bell Beaker architecture is dominated by smaller structures, between 5 to 7 m wide and from 10 to 20 m long. Only twenty or so actual buildings are known from over 100 domestic sites, the majority of which are almond or pear-shaped (Nicolas et al. 2019). Their distribution is biased towards Brittany (Tinévez 2022), although rare examples are recorded in Normandy and Charente. Most of these buildings date to between 2430 and 2150 calBC and are thus not directly associated with the earliest Bell Beaker horizon. For instance, the site of Anse de la République, in Vendée, has recently been redated to the 25th and 24th centuries BC (Gandois et al. 2020). This site is of particular interest as it has yielded direct evidence of copper metallurgy in the form of beaker sherds used as crucibles, which have direct parallels on other western French sites (e.g., Les Florentins: Billard et al. 1998).

The events unfolding in Atlantic France during the late 3rd millennium calBC matter not only because they provide a geographical bridge between both putative homelands but more fundamentally because they demonstrate how much connectivity is a central feature of the Bell Beaker Phenomenon for its entire duration. Funerary similarities linking this space to the Low Countries are not restricted to a narrow early temporal horizon but occur over several centuries. Further, it is also noteworthy how practices initiated during this period (e.g., preference for arrowheads as grave goods) impacted the development of the succeeding Early Bronze Age.

3.4 Central Europe

Central Europe has always enjoyed an awkward status in Bell Beaker studies: rarely considered as a potential homeland, yet seen as a driving force, this area provides some of the highest regional concentrations of finds of the entire domain. One of the key elements in this discussion relates to the assessment of the legacy of the cultural substrate known as the Corded Ware Complex in this sequence.

The Corded Ware Complex is well-known in Later European prehistory for its combination of broad geographic distribution, relative lack of settlement evidence, and highly patterned funerary practices, most burials being individual graves with bodies laid on an east–west axis facing south, men lay on their right side and women on their left. However, as demonstrated by Furholt (e.g., Furholt 2014), behind this apparent homogeneity lies a tapestry of regional variation. The archaeological fame of this complex has also been raised within archaeological ranks – and most unfortunately beyond (e.g., Hakenbeck 2019) – by its association with high-profile aDNA studies and findings. As previously mentioned, samples dated to this period demonstrate the introduction of a new genomic component in the genetic variation of Europe, the so-called steppe ancestry (Allentoft et al. 2015; Haak et al. 2015). Despite decades of discussion on the presence, or lack of, migration during this period, these studies were met by a range of reactions ranging from devoted support (e.g., Kristiansen et al. 2017) to cautious criticism (e.g., Vander Linden 2016; Furholt 2018). A few years on, new studies and samples, unsurprisingly, given the limited size and geographical spread of the original studies, point to more complexity than was suggested by the original claim of massive migrations. Re-examination of the original data led to identification of sex bias in the migratory movement, pointing to an imbalance in favour of men (Goldberg et al. 2017a). Fiercely debated at first (Lazaridis & Reich 2017, and countered by Golberg et al. 2017b), this interpretation has found empirical support in regional studies (e.g., Saag et al. 2017). In Moravia, Papac and colleagues report high levels of steppe ancestry in Corded Ware individuals of both sexes, but also four women without any trace of it at all, as well as the inception of another genetic ancestry linked to the forest zone, thus pointing to a mixture of individuals from various geographical origins and local populations all contributing to the gene pool (Papac et al. 2021). Interestingly, they also report shifts in genetic diversity over time in the course of the Corded Ware Complex, a welcome reminder that archaeological complexes are dynamic processes and should never be reduced to static ethnographic-like snapshots.

In light of these points, it is easy to see how and why the Corded Ware Complex and the Bell Beaker Phenomenon are sometimes seen as archaeological siblings. This impression is reinforced by their geographic and chronological overlap. Regarding the latter, the image of a typological chest of drawers, whereby one culture simply succeeds another, has sometimes been invoked to account for the Corded Ware-Bell Beaker sequence. Many elements, however, indicate that this perception is misleading and that face-to-face interactions between the producers and bearers of these respective material cultures effectively happened. Such encounters are implicitly at the core of Sangmeister's Rückstrom theory to account for typological traits of assumed Corded descendent traits in later Bell Beaker assemblages. Setting such typological presuppositions aside, occurrences of graves of both cultures in the same cemeteries have long been reported, but the best demonstration of the effective contemporaneity of both complexes comes from settlement evidence. Recent excavation and survey programmes conducted in development-led contexts in the Saale and Elbe river valleys of central Germany have demonstrated the co-existence of both complexes between 2500 and 2200 calBC, characterized by distinctive architectural traditions and settlement patterns (Risch et al. 2022; see also Spatzier and Schumke 2019; Strahm 2019). Bell Beaker buildings present a trapezoidal shape roughly comparable to the Corded Ware examples, though the latter are generally wider. More significantly, while Corded Ware sites are found on high, grazing grounds, Bell Beaker ones are preferentially located on agricultural lands closer to the rivers. All in all, at least for this region, one can firmly speak of two communities living side-by-side, using different material cultures, practising related yet diverging burial rituals (see below), and exploiting different parts of the landscape.

Settlement evidence has always been the documentary weakest link for the Bell Beaker Phenomenon, thus contributing to its identification with wandering pastoralist peoples, a vision which provides a simplistic mechanism to account for its large-scale distribution. However, as the previous example shows, the empirical situation has improved over the past few decades, and even though building plans remain scarce, the number of domestic sites has steadily increased as has our knowledge of regional Bell Beaker settlement patterns. The Bell Beaker situation just described for the Elbe–Saale river valley differs from the Lake Constance region, where Corded Ware settlements are located by the lake, alongside the low-lying hinterland for pasture, while the shores are abandoned during the Bell Beaker phase in favour of the higher Hegau region (Lechterbeck et al. 2014). In Moravia and Bohemia, the distribution of findspots suggests networks of small settlements, located close to rivers and with access to pastureland given the primacy of cattle in the zooarchaeological assemblages (c. 70% on average: Turek 2019). Preferential use of low terraces and lowlands is also noted in eastern Austria, with the notable mention of two boat-shaped houses on the site of Walpersdorf, and a high proportion of horse bones at Vienna 3 (Kern et al. 2019). Use of river terraces, boat-shaped houses, and faunal assemblages dominated by horse remains are recurrent features in the central Hungarian Bell Beaker–Csepel group in central Hungary (Reményi et al. 2019).

The bulk of the evidence for the central European Bell Beaker still comes from the funerary sphere, with individual graves found isolated, in small groups, or in cemeteries organised in rows. These graves also famously follow strict rules, with bodies being generally aligned on a north–south axis, men lying on their left side facing east, and women in a symmetrical position on their right side, facing east. Though reminiscent of the Corded Ware rules, it is noteworthy that, in order to move from one pattern to the other, one has to apply two geometric transformations: a rotational and a reflectional symmetry. Arguably both Corded Ware and Bell Beaker practices present a much wider range of variation, but the necessity of applying these two transformations points to shared conceptions underlying both funerary conceptions. Another widely encountered practice in central European Bell Beaker graves reinforces the importance of gender in the funerary ideology: once more keeping in mind the existence of numerous exceptions, men tend to be buried with drinking vessels and weapons, especially echoing the world of archery, and women with drinking and other vessels. Much has been written on this topic (e.g., Turek 2013; Müller 2001), and in view of the overall objectives of this element, the key thing here is to stress that, overall, gendered disposal rules were important, though their regional implementation varied extensively.

The examination of grave goods provides further information regarding the rules governing mortuary practices. Bell beakers in funerary contexts are often the main drinking vessel in a grave, though in some cases, handled cups are used as a substitute (Besse 2003; Figure 11). Stone bracers – worn on the forearm – are another common feature in graves, especially male ones. These artefacts present extensive variations in raw material, colour, and morphology (e.g., number of perforations ranging from two to six), and technological analysis suggests limited knowledge involved in their making, thus possibly indicating personal production (Nicolas 2020). Several examples of reshaping or redrilling of the perforations indicate that these bracers were effectively worn, although use-wear analysis does not support their assumed function as archers' wrist-guards (Nicolas 2020; Fokkens et al. 2008). By comparison, the relationship between arrowheads and archery is unquestionable. Regional variation occurs here as well, although at a much larger scale. Corresponding to the barbed and tanged specimens of western Europe, in central Europe we see arrowheads with concave bases delineating two distinctive wings (Bailly 2014). Geometric morphometrical analysis of Moravian examples suggests a low typological diversity, amplified by minor micro-regional variation in terms of raw material use (Petřík et al. 2018). Interestingly, there are few known broken examples, suggesting that these arrowheads were part of arrow shafts made and deposited on purpose in the graves (Petřík et al. 2018).

Other dimensions of the funerary record point to further (micro-)regional variation. For instance, cremations are frequent in the central Hungarian Csepel group, but otherwise use of fire in the mortuary context is infrequent. Another example, though not a cremation as such, is provided by a couple of graves excavated at Altwies – Op dem Boesch, in present-day Luxemburg (Le Brun-Ricalens et al. 2011). The first grave contained the remains of a single individual, while the second included those of an adult, most likely a woman, and a three- to four-year-old child. Both burials followed the same sequence of events: after digging the pit, a hearth was lit at the bottom, and then the bottom surface was carefully cleaned prior to the deposition of the dead. Eventually the graves were sealed using some form of solid lid. The existence of funerary chambers and/or multiple burials is actually documented across central Europe, but especially at its western periphery. Located less than a 100 km from Altwies, the site of Pouilly has yielded another example of a double grave covered by a wooden lid (Lefebvre et al. 2011). Here, the human remains included those of an individual buried according to the traditional central European Bell Beaker pattern, as well as long bones and a skull, possibly collected in a box. Nearby, at Hatrize, French archaeologists have reconstructed an entire wooden chamber containing the burial of an adult individual, a three- to five-year-old child, and a cremation. This tradition of funerary chambers is also documented by several examples at Mondelange (Lefebvre et al. 2008).

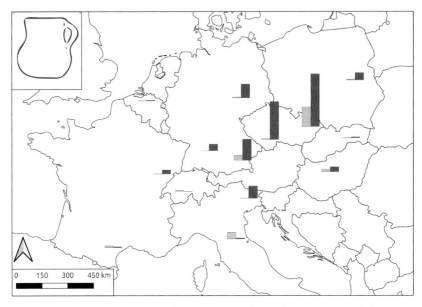

Figure 12 Proportion of handled cups in settlement and burials
(data from Besse 2003).

Such wooden chambers are not the sole expression of funerary architecture in this part of the Bell Beaker domain. Located at its geographical margins, the site of Petit-Chasseur, in the Swiss western Alps, exemplifies several key Bell Beaker traits. Built and first used as a collective burial in the Late Neolithic alongside anthropomorphic stelae, this monument was emptied, reused, and partially rebuilt during the Bell Beaker period (Figure 12). This phase of activity is famous for the creation of richly decorated anthropomorphic stelae, with an intricate iconography displaying the importance of archery and martiality for their creators (Harrison & Heyd 2007). Monumentality remains a rare feature in the central European Bell Beaker landscape, aside from a handful of examples. In this context the recent discovery of a monumental complex at Pömmelte is as stunning as it is exceptional (Spatzier & Bertemes 2018). Located in Saxony-Anhalt, this circular enclosure of c.100 m diameter combines several concentric ditches and posts circles. Bayesian modelling of 14C dates places the beginning of the building activity around 2450 to 2200 calBC, followed by two successive phases of occupation, until deconstruction in the 21st century calBC, a phase linked to the Early Bronze Age Únětice culture. This complex monument includes several categories of deposits. The earliest – Bell Beaker – involved not only the creation of the enclosure itself but also the digging of shaft-like pits for deposition of various kinds of material culture, animal bones, as well as

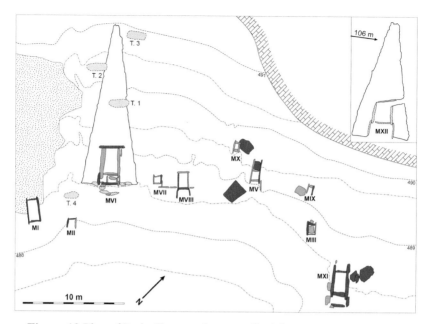

Figure 13 Plan of Petit-Chasseur I necropolis (after Carloni et al. 2023).

'deviant' human burials, many of them showing signs of inter-personal violence. While unique in central Europe, such a range of construction, use and
ritual activity strongly echoes contemporary sites from southern Britain, raising
the question of possible direct connections between these two areas.

As interesting, though more modest in size, is Brodek in Czechia (Gašpar et al.
2023; Figure 13). Another recent discovery, this site has yielded a set of four
grave-like pits organised in a rectangular pattern, coupled with two parallel rows
of nine postholes. None of the four pits contained human remains, but each was
associated with a specific range of material culture reminiscent of grave goods,
for instance arrowheads, stone bracers, and ornaments in structure 1, tools for
metalworking (cushion stones) in structure 2, and many pottery types in all of
them. Several of these pots presented incised decoration, filled by a white inlay.
This decorative trait, widely observed across the area, is a post-firing treatment
which was obtained using a range of raw materials including kaolin, bone, or
gypsum. Across the Morava river valley catchment, this technology presents
some micro-regional variation, alluding to the existence of local pottery traditions
(Všianský et al. 2014). At Brodek, provenance study of this white inlay indicates
a mixture of local and non-local sources, with up to a quarter of the assemblages
deriving from places 15 to 55 km away, thus suggesting that the site could have
attracted communities originating from a variety of places.

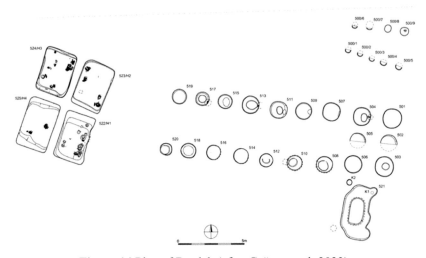

Figure 14 Plan of Brodek (after Gašpar et al. 2023).

While the movement of individuals across the landscape, for instance to potential ritual gathering sites, is interesting in its own right, undeniably the focus over the past ten years has been on relocation and migration. Pioneering work by Price and colleagues on central European sites suggested a relatively high level of mobility, but no clear patterning in terms of gender, though there was a slightly higher proportion of women who had undertaken relocation over the course of their lifetimes (Price et al. 1998, 2004). Further studies have confirmed these results, with changing levels of mobility and a trend towards preferential movement of women over men. Joint aDNA and isotopic sampling of thirty-four individuals in the cemeteries of Alburg and Irlbach have identified eight non-locals, six of them women (Sjögren et al. 2020). This last trait is reinforced by a high level of mitochondrial DNA diversity, contrasting with homogeneity for the Y-chromosome. Noticeably, extensive amounts of first-degree relationships between individuals were recorded on both sites, pointing to the importance of kinship ties in the making of funerary communities. Similar results in terms of high mtDNA variation were also observed for several sites in the Lech valley, in south-western Germany (Knipper et al. 2017; Mittnik et al. 2019). The number of outliers identified by strontium analyses for this region is not straightforward, as only one woman presents an isotopic signature markedly different from the local baseline, with a further two women and one man less certain. Arguably, strontium analysis only provides a minimum number of individuals flagged as non-locals (as individuals moving within the same bioavailable strontium area would not be identified). It is essential, however, to stress the uncertainty inherent in these analytical techniques, especially in contrast with the simplicity of interpretative models stressing the role of post-marital residency rules (see Section 4).

At the population level, Olalde and colleagues' study (2018) highlighted the presence of steppe ancestry amongst central European Bell Beaker individuals, and the lack of discernible ancestry out of Iberia, challenging earlier results based on uniparental makers (Brandt et al. 2013; Brotherton et al. 2013). More recent work has systematically pointed to a higher level of Neolithic farming ancestry in Bell Beaker samples than in Corded Ware ones, suggesting admixture with local groups (e.g., Mittnik et al. 2019; Papac et al. 2021). Papac and collaborators also reported differences in Y-chromosome variation and lineages between the Corded Ware, central European Bell Beaker, and British Bell Beaker samples, highlighting the demographic diversity of the phenomenon (Papac et al. 2021).

As in the Netherlands, the Bell Beaker Phenomenon in central Europe is more than a mere temporal continuity of Corded Ware traits, with a complex population history, and new trends in both settlement pattern and funerary practices. However, especially regarding the latter, it remains clear that the vocabulary and framework established during the Corded Ware period constituted a key reference for Bell Beaker practices.

3.5 Western Mediterranean Basin

The cultural landscape of the Western Mediterranean basin, excluding the Iberian Peninsula previously covered, is marked, on the one hand, by a variety of local ceramic traditions, and on the other by widely shared funerary practices such as collective burials, though with some regional diversity. The Late Neolithic of southern France presents a dazzlingly complex terminology, mirroring blends of typological traits, technological traditions, and likely small-scale population movements (e.g., Pétrequin 1993; Cauliez 2011). At the same time, the funerary landscape is dominated by collective burials set in multiple contexts, with a noticeably high frequency of cases of interpersonal violence (Guilaine & Zammit 2001). Other expressions of violence, such as the diversity and quantity of arrowheads (Remicourt et al. 2018), and of masculinity (as seen in ornaments: Barge 1982; see also Maréchal et al. 1998), all contribute to an ambiance of increased intra-group social tension and competition. Though, to a lesser extent, the Italian sequence also exhibits a relative diversity of cultural traditions, the most notable feature is the rise of martial ideologies, especially in the funerary realm (Dolfini 2022). Lastly, it is worth noting that the western Mediterranean basin witnesses the onset of copper metallurgy during the late 4th and early 3rd millennium calBC, with traces of mining and smelting at several locations, and extensive consumption evidenced in both domestic and funerary contexts (e.g., Ambert & Carozza 1996; Dolfini 2014).

The extent and nature of Bell Beaker expressions vary greatly across the Western Mediterranean basin, from a high density of sites across southern France to patches in the Balearic Islands, Sardinia, Sicily, and the Tyrrhenian coast, and near-complete absence in Corsica and the Adriatic basin. As in the preceding period, collective burials of varying size and architecture (e.g., dolmens, hypogea, small caves) remain the norm, with several instances of reuse of existing sites during the Bell Beaker period (e.g., Lemercier & Tchéréminisoff 2011; Melis 2019). Individual burials remain rare, for instance a newborn burial at La Grotte-Murée (Courtin et al. 2011) and the site of La Fare. The latter grave, dated to the first centuries of the Bell Beaker chronology (c. 2450–2280 calBC), belongs to a man, buried with a beaker, several other pots, a likely locally produced copper dagger. It was found in the middle of a settlement otherwise characterised by material culture belonging to the local Rhône-Ouvèze ceramic group. All evidence suggests that this could correspond to the burial of a 'foreigner' within a local environment (Lemercier et al. 2011). This interpretation seems to be confirmed by the high proportion of steppe ancestry identified for this individual (c. 58 per cent: Olalde et al. 2018; Patterson et al. 2021). Across most of Italy, funerary Bell Beaker finds remain exceptional, with a single sherd in over a hundred tombs in central Italy (Dolfini 2019), a potential barrow associated with domestic remains at Via Bruschi (Sarti et al. 2012), and the deposition of human remains with Bell Beaker pottery and a wristguard at Fosso Connochio (Dolfini 2009).

Settlements are relatively well documented in southern France and northern Italy, far less so in other areas. A recurring feature in southern France, as just noted for La Fare, is the presence of Bell Beaker finds in sites otherwise characterised by the material culture of local traditions, leading to a distinction between so-called Bell Beaker sites and sites with bell beakers, echoing the situation for the Iberian Peninsula (Lemercier et al. 2019). Settlements are found in all sorts of topographical settings, but with some regional preferences (e.g., hilltops in western Provence). As in other parts of the domain, architectural features and structures remain rare (Lemercier et al. 2019). Northern Italy presents a relative concentration of domestic sites. Regional diversity is the rule, with caves, rock shelters, and marshlands all favoured, as well as alluvial plains, sometimes with clusters of sites in specific river valleys (Baioni et al. 2019).

While strontium and ancient DNA sampling remain very limited in comparison to other parts of Europe, the inception of steppe ancestry seems to be later here than in central and northern Europe (Brunel et al. 2020), although modelling of the few available genomic sequences suggests this event dates to c. 2600–2500 calBC in southern France, contemporary with the earliest local Bell Beaker phase (Seguin-Orlando et al. 2021). It is worth pointing out the occurrence, at the same time, of individuals without any traces of steppe ancestry. The onset of steppe ancestry in the Balearic Islands, probably from Iberia, dates to 2400 calBC, in Sicily to 2200 calBC with the same likely source, and to the 2nd mill calBC in Sardinia (Fernandes et al. 2020). For Italy, the few existing samples indicate the presence of steppe ancestry by the last centuries of the 3rd millennium calBC, though this genomic signature is not confined to individuals from Bell Beaker cultural contexts (Saupe et al. 2021).

Although areas such as southern France and northern Italy are certainly rich in Bell Beaker finds and sites, it is hard not to conclude that the Western Mediterranean basin sits in a peripheral position, either physically, culturally, or genetically, compared to the rest of the Bell Beaker Phenomenon.

3.6 Britain and Ireland

The cultural, social, and economic picture in Britain for the first half of the 3rd millennium BC is best described in terms of mobile, yet inward-looking processes, though with instances of interactions across the Irish Sea. While famous sites such as Skara Brae testify to the architectural richness in Scotland and nearby islands, settlements remain rare and are confined to pit scatters across most of England (Bradley 2019: 88–149). Together with the scarcity of cereals in archaeobotanical assemblages, several scholars see this period as one dominated by pastoralism and an overall low population density, although the local validity of this interpretation remains debated (Stevens & Fuller 2012; Bishop 2015). Not much information is available on the funerary world either, aside from a few cremation cemeteries (e.g., Parker Pearson et al. 2009; Noble et al. 2017). By far the most significant traits are, across most of the island, the occurrence of the Grooved Ware ceramic tradition, and the emphasis upon monuments and monumental landscapes (e.g., Thomas 2010). These last two elements also occur in parts of Ireland, though its cultural trajectory remains markedly different in several respects such as the continuing importance of megalithic architecture and other funerary practices (Bradley 2019: 88–149). Noticeably, the high level of interaction across the Irish Sea is not mirrored by the movement of goods, ideas, or people across the Channel and the North Sea, or at least nothing which left any conspicuous traces in the archaeological record; Britain seems isolated from the many changes happening on the contemporary continent (Wilkin & Vander Linden 2015).

The situation radically changes in the 25th century BC with the arrival of the Bell Beaker Phenomenon and transformations in many facets of the archaeological record. Burial practices offer the most striking evidence of this upheaval; the stereotypical image of the individual crouched burial placed under a barrow holds a certain truth, as hundreds of such sites feature prominently across British landscapes. However, as recently discussed by Bloxam and Parker Pearson (2022), other practices such as disarticulation and cremation repeatedly occur before, during, and after the Bell Beaker phase across all of the British regions. Gender-based rules regarding the disposal of the body and of grave goods are recorded across Britain although with an extensive degree of regional variation (Shepherd 2012). Beakers, arrowheads, varied ornaments, and wristguards feature prominently in funerary assemblages, sometimes in exceptional quantities as in the case of the Amesbury Archer (Fitzpatrick 2013). Arguably, these traits present clear antecedents in continental Europe, but, at the same time and as seems to be the norm during the Bell Beaker period, they all reflect extensive local reinterpretation by British communities. This process is evident in ceramic decoration, and in particular after 2300 calBC, the so-called fission horizon is marked by a multiplicity of local styles (Needham 2005; Parker Pearson et al. 2019). Stone wristguards tell a similar tale. Morphologically and technologically, these compare well with their continental prototypes, but, in terms of raw material, it is noticeable that several examples share common lithology with Neolithic axes, as both traditions sourced their raw material from Langdale volcanic stuff (Woodward et al. 2006, 2011). The use of such a specific local raw material indicates a high level of familiarity with available lithological sources by the makers, and possibly users, of these objects.

The key area of British Bell Beaker cultural exceptionalism is monuments. Henges as well as stone and timber circles were already central to the ritual world of pre-Beaker populations, with extensive evidence of feasting and movement of animals to such sites (e.g., Madgwick et al. 2019). Ongoing Bell Beaker activity on several monumental sites demonstrates continuity between both periods. Examples largely drawn from south-western Britain include a deposition phase at the mega-henge of Mount Pleasant (Greaney et al. 2020), the building of Silbury Hill, a solid mound of turf and chalk (Bayliss et al. 2007) in the Avebury complex, and a new phase of construction at Stonehenge (Darvill et al. 2009). The latter also acts as a visual point of reference in the landscape, with several barrows, such as that of the Amesbury Archer, erected on the surrounding horizon line or in its near vicinity during the Bell Beaker Period and the succeeding Early Bronze Age (e.g., Needham et al. 2010).

By contrast with the architectural extravaganza of monuments, data on settlements and particularly houses remain scanty. Noticeably, this evidential state of affairs has hardly changed even after recent and extensive commercial work, suggesting that we are dealing here with a real pattern and not an artefact of modern rescue archaeology (Gibson 2019a). The few known house buildings, all dry stone-walled houses, come from the Hebridean islands, while across Britain, settlements take the form of few features such as pits or stakeholes, and/or surface materials (Gibson 2019b). Available zooarchaeological remains point to an apparent importance of cattle, a pattern also suggested by extensive cattle deposits in funerary contexts in Irthlingborough and Gayhurst (Towers et al. 2010). Despite this paucity of settlements, the Bell Beaker period, especially its later phases, seems linked to a new uptick in agricultural intensification, which was to last into the Middle Bronze Age (Stevens & Fuller 2012).

Britain has one of the most extensive strontium and ancient DNA samples, giving us a unique window into the complexity of mobility patterns, and the vagaries of aligning the results of both techniques. Strontium analyses conducted across the island point to a minimal proportion of c. 30 per cent of non-local individuals, a relatively stable figure across time. Regional variation occurs but is likely to be related to the resolution of the technique and local underlying geology rather than to past divergences in human behaviour (Parker Pearson et al. 2019; Figure 15). Examples of long-distance movements, such as the Amesbury Archer, however, are very rare. This last result contrasts with those gained from ancient DNA, which indicates a large-scale migration from the continent associated with the onset of the Bell Beaker Phenomenon (Olalde et al. 2018). While the existence of such migration is undeniable, assessing its structure is more difficult. Olalde and colleagues (2018) originally suggested a population turnover of more than 90 per cent by the Middle Bronze Age. Further work demonstrates that we need to go beyond this astounding – and frankly controversial – number. For instance, the genetic make-up of the incoming population was fairly complex, with the Amesbury Archer for instance presenting a low level of steppe ancestry (Patterson et al. 2021). Careful examination also indicates a higher proportion of individuals with local Neolithic ancestry during the closing centuries of the 3rd millennium calBC (Booth et al. 2021; Figure 16). In this sense, the mismatch between strontium and ancient DNA does not lie so much in the fact that the former can only identify so-called first-generation migrants, a point often stressed by strong advocates of aDNA research (e.g., Armit and Reich 2021). It rather seems that, after the initial population movement, frequent but spatially limited mobility took place within Britain, including through post-marital residency rules. The associated genetic shuffling must have contributed to the overall demographic structure of this population, although the details remain unclear

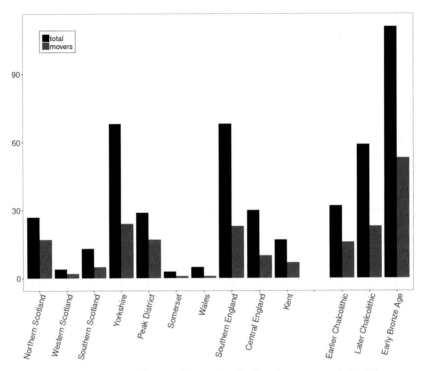

Figure 15 Sr data for UK (data after Parker Pearson et al. 2019).

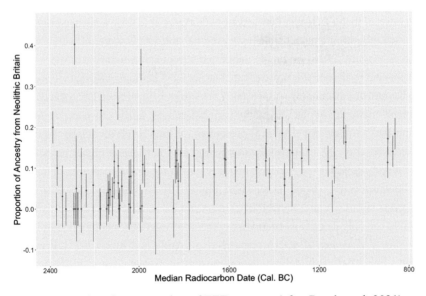

Figure 16 Changing proportion of EEF ancestry (after Booth et al. 2021).

(see also Booth et al. 2021). On that note, it is noteworthy that ancient DNA has also proven long suspected family ties between individuals buried under the same mound or barrow, although the emerging picture is far from clearly patterned (Booth et al. 2021).

Although Britain and Ireland are tackled here together given their geographical proximity, their cultural trajectory and identity within the Bell Beaker Phenomenon are far from identical (Carlin 2018). Only two aspects of the Irish manifestation of the BBP echo the British situation: firstly, poorly known domestic architecture, with the settlement record only yielding pits, artefacts spreads, and very few postholes and stakeholes; secondly, presence of Bell Beaker material culture on monuments such as timber circles. The funerary domain sees the reuse of older monumental tombs, and the development of a new megalithic architectural type, wedge tombs, which contain a combination of cremation, collective burials, and possible successive individual burials (Carlin 2018). Another key trait of the Irish Bell Beaker sequence is copper metallurgy, with the founding of and continuous activity at the Ross Island copper mine (O'Brien 2004). This site supplied the majority of copper in Ireland and Britain for several centuries (e.g., Bray & Pollard 2012), with exports also known along the entire Atlantic coast (e.g., Gandois et al. 2019). Lastly, although sampling remains limited to a handful of Early Bronze Age individuals, steppe ancestry was introduced to Ireland during the Bell Beaker period (Cassidy et al. 2016).

Ireland thus remains in a somewhat peripheral position within the Bell Beaker sphere, and this is in spite of extensive economic contacts as indicated by the widespread occurrence of Ross Island copper. Britain, for its part, clearly appears as a Bell Beaker–rich area, marked by a profound transformation of the funerary world, mirrored by extensive reshaping of the genomic landscape. At the same time, Britain's trajectory is by no means a mere extension of nearby north-western continental Europe, with continuity in monumental occupation and construction, and local reinterpretation of many traits.

3.7 Northern Europe

The last region considered in this short overview is northern Europe, where the Bell Beaker Phenomenon succeeds regional groups of the Corded Ware Complex. Some of the key elements noted in the previous pages, such as individual burials or the introduction of steppe ancestry, are well in place by the time Bell Beaker traits enter the local archaeological record. It is also worth remembering that, especially when compared to the rest of the BBP, the northernmost Bell Beaker groups start late in the sequence, that is, no earlier than 2350 calBC, if not later.

The highest regional density of finds and sites comes from Jutland and concerns the domestic realm. For the Late Neolithic I (2350–1950 calBC), Sarauw mentions no less than 340 houses from 160 sites, of which 100 houses in 48 sites are identified as Bell Beaker (Sarauw 2019). The majority of those present a sunken end which, unlike Medieval examples, was unlikely to have been used as a byre but was rather dedicated to other functions such as grain storage or processing (Simonsen 2018). From a mortuary point of view, there is clear continuity with the dominant individual burial rite. Interestingly, and in contrast with other European regions, bell beakers are absent from funerary inventories. However, numerous graves, whose distribution overlaps with that of Bell Beaker settlements, have yielded daggers and arrowheads, possibly related to an ideological influence from the rest of the Bell Beaker domain (Sarauw 2007). Further north in Norway, several finds, including at least one beaker but also several barbed-and-tanged arrowheads and wristguards, point to either a direct Bell Beaker presence or at least some interaction with Jutland communities (e.g., Prescott 2020). This was a process unfolding against a background of profound socioeconomic transformation marked by the full transition to agriculture and a related demographic explosion (Solheim 2021; Figure 17).

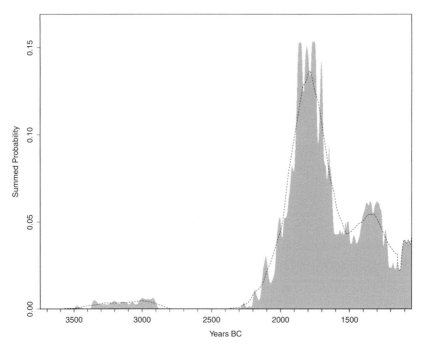

Figure 17 SPDs of directly dated cereal samples for Norway (data from Solheim 2021).

Direct information on Bell Beaker mobility and genomic ancestry for this region remains limited. Steppe ancestry was introduced parallel to the Corded Ware Complex, an event which profoundly reshaped the genomic diversity of the region (Egfjord et al. 2021). Results only available as a preprint at the time of writing suggest further fine-grained changes in the ancestry profile of Danish individuals between the Late Neolithic and the Early Bronze Age, thus post-dating the local Bell Beaker sequence (Allentoft et al. 2024). Likewise, a Neolithic–Bronze Age transect of strontium analysis of human samples points to a continuous low proportion of outliers across all Neolithic periods, with profound changes only occurring from 1600 calBC onwards (Frei et al. 2019).

Although clearly set in a geographical and cultural periphery, the dynamics of this region encapsulate the kaleidoscopic variation which has accompanied this journey across the Bell Beaker Phenomenon. The presence of Bell Beaker material culture is itself subject to tremendous variation as, for instance, in cases where beakers are absent from the funerary sphere but are dominant in the domestic one. Even in such cases a martial dimension can be observed in mortuary practices, another recurrent trait, though reflecting a myriad of local versions and reinterpretations. The question remains: Is there any harmony to be found within this difference? The following section answers with a resounding yes, though to get there a detour via population ecology is required.

4 The Emergence of a Metapopulation?

Imagine an idealised, simplistic landscape composed of spatially discrete habitats, some unoccupied, some hosting a single population. Assume also that the demographic history of each group is relatively independent (i.e., prone to random fluctuations), although all populations interact together to some extent, for instance, through the movement of individuals. In such a model, while each group follows its own trajectory and thus eventually goes extinct, the entire set of populations considered together, referred to as a metapopulation, will remain stable thanks to the continuous flow of individuals between patches. For example, a given group may grow and repopulate an abandoned patch or bring in new individuals to a population on the brink of collapse (e.g., Levins 1969; Hanski & Ovaskainen 2003).

This is known in population ecology as a metapopulation model and was formalised in 1969 by Richard Levins to originally account for insect pests in agricultural fields (Levins 1969). Since then, this model has been applied to numerous ecological contexts and refined in several ways (e.g., Ovaskainen & Saastamoinen 2018). One improvement particularly relevant for our purpose is the addition of habitat properties. In its original formulation, the model assumes

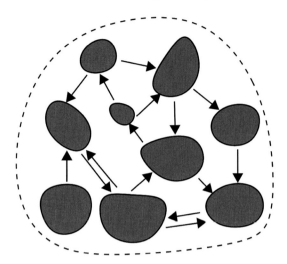

Figure 18 diagrammatic illustration of metapopulation models. In this version, all patches are populated and interconnected.

that the landscape is homogeneous, that is, that all patches are qualitatively equal. In such cases, the degree of connectivity between patches is dependent upon the distance between them. Obviously, in real life this assumption is rarely, if ever, met. More recent versions of the models therefore consider habitat fragmentation, so that each habitat has its own properties, which in turn impact the behaviour and eventual demographic history of the population inhabiting it (e.g., Hanski & Ovaikanen 2003).

One may wonder why this digression, and what a model drawn from theoretical population ecology can contribute to our goal in this volume. The argument developed in this section is that the Bell Beaker Phenomenon constitutes a metapopulation (Figure 19), a structure not only unprecedented in Later European prehistory but which also constitutes the framework for the key dynamics of the succeeding Bronze Age.

The suggested identity rests upon two points. Firstly, the spatially discontinuous patterning of habitats in the theoretical model matches the patchwork of heterogeneous regional Bell Beaker groups. As seen in Section 2, one of the key traits of this spatial structure lies in its latitudinal spread, and thus the multiplicity of environments and landscapes occupied by Bell Beaker communities. Further, these diverse patches do not constitute a continuous territory, with the nature of the blank areas in-between having also been explored in Section 2. Secondly, and as a correlate of the first point, just as the theoretical ecological model relies upon the movement of individuals between patches to ensure the long-term stability of the overall metapopulation, our review of the evidence

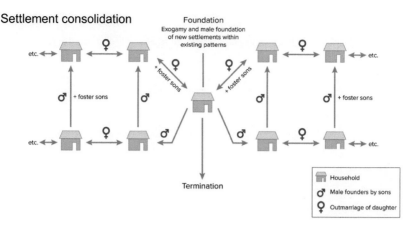

Figure 19 Sjögren and colleagues' model of social institutions and associated mobility patterns for the Bell Beaker Phenomenon (after Sjögren et al. 2020).

has shown that all regions exhibit varying levels of human mobility. Stressing the role of migration and post-marital rules is hardly original in view of the recent data, but the argument here is to generalise the suggestion that connectivity is instrumental to both the creation and the maintenance of the Bell Beaker Phenomenon. It is this process which marks a qualitative difference between pre- and post-Bell Beaker in the general trajectory of Later European Prehistory, an essential point which the concept of metapopulation helps to identify and further explore.

Yet, if we keep the description at such a general level, would it not be simpler and possibly more accurate to speak of the Bell Beaker Phenomenon as a network, instead of resorting to such a specific ecological model? Formally speaking, a metapopulation constitutes a network, where each patch is a node, and where the corridors connecting the patches correspond to the vertices. However, while a metapopulation is always a network, the reverse proposition is not necessarily true as the assumptions associated with each diverge profoundly. Network analysis has gained a certain level of attention in archaeological thought (e.g., Collar et al. 2015) and has been used to describe sets of relationships between individual sites in a variety of settings, including Bell Beaker ones (e.g., Kleijne 2019; Caraglio 2020). Drawing such a network relies upon selecting one or several traits to measure similarity between nodes, and while pottery typology is often favoured, other items have also been taken into consideration (e.g., Bourgeois & Kroon 2017). The key difference between network analysis and the metapopulation model lies in the nature of the vertices. Network analysis can be used to conceptualise and visualise the effects of various processes (e.g., trade, interaction), with the assumption that higher similarity between nodes reflects increased levels of contact (Collar et al. 2015). By contrast, in a metapopulation, the movement of individuals is the sole mechanism linking patches and thus a property of the system more than a mere attribute. In this sense, if any archaeological culture could theoretically be described and analysed as a network, the same does not hold in metapopulation terms.

The possible identification of the Bell Beaker Phenomenon as a metapopulation raises the question of the origins of this particular structure. Do pre-existing interaction networks explain the Bell Beaker Phenomenon, and, if not, how do we qualify the different state of affairs pertaining in the first and second halves of the 3rd millennium calBC? As seen in Section 3, lots of things and lots of people are moving around Europe during the centuries, leading up to the Bell Beaker Phenomenon: Grooved Ware and monuments across Britain and the Irish Sea, amber and ivory flowing – albeit in likely small quantities – in Iberia, Grand-Pressigny daggers being exchanged along stretches of the French Atlantic coast, and migrations within the Corded Ware Complex. And yet, the overall impression is one of fragmentation given the general small scale of these networks, with the notable exception of the Corded Ware Complex, although how this migratory flow translates into material homogeneity is open to question (Furholt 2014). This sum of limited connections is supported by a variety of artefacts, raw materials, and humans so that, eventually, it is impossible to reconstruct a cohesive mesh. Further, when compared to the Bell Beaker distribution, this mesh would also present several gaps, such as the apparent lack of cross-Channel contacts. During the Bell Beaker Phenomenon, artefacts are unsurprisingly also being exchanged, though the scale and nature of this process are open to debate. Archaeometric programmes aimed at testing the prestige hypothesis have repeatedly shown that, while there are undeniable instances of bell beakers being traded, these remain a minority. Thus, transfer of knowledge, often leading to local reinterpretation, is a more compelling explanation for their widespread distribution, one that seems to be valid for other components of the Bell Beaker package, as exemplified by British stone bracers for instance.

Taking into consideration material culture only, there are thus clear indications that human mobility, as the vector for such suggested knowledge and technological transfer, plays a key role in the making of the Bell Beaker Phenomenon. Until recently, such movement was generally envisaged as the being due to the travels of craftspeople (e.g., Prieto-Martinez & Salanova 2009), in some ways echoing Childe's old idea of wandering smiths. Over the past two decades, such a limited view of human mobility has been radically transformed by the growing body of strontium and especially ancient DNA research.

However, there is a wide and frightening gulf between, on the one hand, the technical sophistication of such studies and, on the other, the shallowness of the theoretical discourse on mobility in archaeology. Numerous studies have begun to fill this problematic gap, ranging from critical assessment of the perceived naivety of ancient DNA scholars to a more proactive attitude that seeks to build appropriate concepts. In regard to the latter, several archaeologists have, as so often is the case in times of epistemological crisis in the discipline, fallen back on ethnographic inspiration or, in a more innovative move, on comparative linguistic data. Arguably, the most articulate version of this last trend can be seen in a contribution by Sjögren and colleagues (2020). Combining isotopic and genomic data from two Austrian Bell Beaker cemeteries with information gained from comparative Indo-European linguistics, they offer a model of social institution relying upon three distinct mechanisms of human mobility: foundation of new settlements by male individuals, female patrilocality (i.e., relocation of married women in the settlement of their husbands), and fosterage of younger boys in their mother's family (Figure 19). This model, however, presents some issues. Without advocating a strict obedience to Popper's epistemology, it must be pointed out that it is empirically difficult to test and thus to falsify the presuppositions. Indeed, the resolution of strontium isotopes implies that a lot of movement is likely to go unnoticed. More crucially, the putative identification of men as outliers would be ambiguous as these could either disprove or prove the model (i.e., matrilocality vs. men as founders). The latter would, ideally, require confirmation by genetic studies (i.e., suggested genetic founders being isotopic outliers as well), a requirement that is, however, not met in the original study. Without even considering that human systems are not formal but present varying degrees of agency, one can see how the level of precision of this model constitutes in equal measures its main appeal and weakness, and thus why its range of application to other well-documented situations is limited (see Booth et al. 2021). The problem lies in its attempt to strictly map onto a given analogy – the reconstructed Indo-European kinship system– on the assumption of implicit historical continuity. More fundamentally, and back to our interest in metapopulations, such precision fails to account for a more fundamental property of human mobility patterns during the Bell Beaker Phenomenon.

Back in 2007, in order to account for the then newly emerging strontium data, I revisited Claude Lévi-Strauss' distinction between restricted and generalised marital exchange systems (Lévi-Strauss 1949; Vander Linden 2007). In a restricted system, the transfer of one individual from one community to another one is paralleled by a reciprocal movement, so that only a couple or very limited number of communities are involved. This system is very common

and possibly accounts for a large proportion of the proliferation of archaeological case studies documenting outliers. In contrast, in a generalised system
reciprocity is delayed and not obligatorily fulfilled by the original receiving
group, thus implying a larger range of communities arranged in chains. In true
structuralist fashion, individual groups matter less in such a system than its
totality. A huge theoretical leap – one I am not willing to consider here – is
required to equate Lévi-Strauss' generalised system and metapopulation, but
both models encapsulate in different terms how much the proteiform, continuous, and somewhat structured flow of individuals between all patches constitutes the hallmark of the Bell Beaker Phenomenon.

All in all, the suggested identity of a metapopulation with the Bell Beaker
Phenomenon accommodates both its unique geographic and material patterning, and the growing body of evidence regarding the many forms of human
mobility in both past and present. Although, in contrast to the theoretical terms
of the model, given that none of the local patches ends up abandoned through
extinction of the local population, the new primary role of human connectivity
also explains how the overall stability of the entire system can occur despite
each patch retaining its individual trajectory (i.e., each local sequence presents
its own uniqueness). It is also noteworthy that this structure, set up during the
Bell Beaker period, remains active in the following centuries as human disper-
sals remain documented through ever-changing levels of genomic ancestry,
though admittedly with varying degrees of spatial and temporal intensity. One
may also wonder to what extent material connectivity, with flows of copper, tin,
and bronze artefacts, does not take over as key parameter in the maintenance of
this structure.

This being said, the presence of a Bell Beaker metapopulation does not
explain how a set of heterogeneous and loosely connected patches ended up
becoming such an integrated structure or, in simple terms: What is the driving
force behind the constitution of the Bell Beaker Phenomenon in the first
instance? Though we have already seen that the pre-existing networks cannot
be considered a strong explanatory factor, the historiography offers us another
list of likely candidates. Could it be linked to a common economy and/or
a technological drive? Or social institutions and, especially, the rise of élites
and social hierarchy? Should we consider a new, persuasive ideology? Or,
simply, the dispersal of one or several communities, characterised and thus
traceable by their genomic profile? The following paragraphs consider each of
these questions separately.

The idea of common economy or shared technological breakthrough stresses
the possibility of a causal factor, with cascading repercussions felt across the
entirety of the social system. For Childe, this role was played by copper

metallurgy. Fast-forward a century later, this proposition does not hold much ground, as copper metallurgy has a millennia-long pedigree, with its presence being demonstrated in numerous local groups several centuries prior to the onset of the Bell Beaker Phenomenon. Likewise, while copper circulation plays a key role in linking several Bell Beaker nodes, we have seen it does not constitute a potent force in the trajectory of the overall process. When considering subsistence techniques and keeping in mind evidential shortcomings, dramatic changes at a local scale do sometimes occur, but the overall picture remains one of great diversity, parallel to the latitudinal and environmental variation. Much has also been written on the potential importance of the 'secondary products revolution' (e.g., Garrido Pena 1997), yet the implementation of this concept remains empirically challenging.

Ideally, one would expect to identify not only clear technological factors but also a linear response in social terms, in the form of increased hierarchy or complexity, with elites controlling resources and access to the new products. If the lack of identifiable economic novelties jeopardises such a simplistic model, one should not, however, discard social complexity as an explanatory variable for the Bell Beaker Phenomenon. After all, the identification of the Bell Beaker package with prestige being expressed and circulated amongst the *nouveaux riches* of the 3rd millennium calBC has played a dominant historiographic role, despite a conspicuous lack of defined independent causes. Discrepancies in the quantity and quality of grave goods between burials do exist, though they remain rare and unpatterned at the global scale of the phenomenon. Looking at the world of the living by contrast, there are some incidental clues to coordinating powers, but these are uncommon and, more importantly, less frequent than for preceding periods in various regions (e.g., Iberian Peninsula). There is perhaps more to be gained by rejecting the idea of a putative social ladder and adopting a more inclusive take on the notion of social institutions. Some scholars have followed such a direction by exploring ideas of post-marital mobility rules and fosterage. Yet, here also, methodological and documentary limits are hard to eschew, as is the general feel of regional variation. All in all, there seems to be no coherent Bell Beaker social order.

Retaining the idea of marriage as a social institution, one can wonder if such a transfer of individuals across communities can only exist through the presence of a shared, cautionary discourse, or ideology. Compared to all other factors listed so far, this one scores highly at first sight. Setting aside exceptional connections as suggested for Pömmelte and its contemporary southern British counterparts, funerary practices constitute the crown jewel of Bell Beaker practices. It might prove ultimately impossible, or at least not advisable, even when resorting to historical or ethnographic analogies, to reconstruct fully the Bell Beaker ideology, but if such a coherent body of knowledge ever existed, it surely incorporated elements of gender, cosmology, and martiality. Following Wentink (2020), the ever-repeated, stereotypical material dimension of these concepts could well have provided the support and medium of expression of a so-called 'social front', a set of loosely shared recognised values enabling and facilitating extensive social interaction which many implicitly assume form the core of the Bell Beaker Phenomenon. This social front may have functioned in accord with specific institutions, such as drinking parties. More fundamentally, as also pointed out by Wentink (2020; see also Vander Linden 2006), the more this framework relied upon general, almost without substance, terms of reference, the easier, and thus the more proteiform, would its local implementations and eventual material – and by extension – archaeological actualisations have been.

If the notion of a common ideology proves the most appealing explanation for the BBP so far, its effective mode of transmission must also be addressed. Should we think in terms of neighbour-to-neighbour interactions, proselytising missionaries, a package introduced by a (large?) population of newcomers? Notwithstanding that these suggestions are not mutually exclusive, the latter is not only the oldest explanation found in the historiography, the gold standard against which all other main theories have been built and evaluated, but also the one that has grabbed the headlines over the past few years. It is today impossible to deny the sheer existence of such population movements, and the Bell Beaker Phenomenon builds on a process initiated earlier in the 3rd millennium calBC with the Corded Ware Complex. And yet, once more, the key lies in regional variation. Some areas such as Britain seem to have been hit by a population tsunami (though closer inspection of the data and recent genomic sequencing paints a more complicated picture: Booth et al. 2021; Patterson et al. 2021), while varying levels and tempos in the inception of steppe ancestry point to a less dramatic migratory flux in other parts of the domain. As Olalde and colleagues have already highlighted (Olalde et al. 2018), there was no homogeneous Bell Beaker folk wandering across Europe. Rather than a single migratory movement, one should envisage a multiplicity of local and regional shuffling of communities, some of which might well be perceived only though in-depth analysis of specific genetic markers (e.g., Dulias et al. 2022).

In the most unsatisfactory way for those seeking a simple explanation, it is clear that each of these factors presents its own relevance, and it would be misleading to consider them in isolation. There might well be some value in ranking these factors in disentangling their respective weight on a region per region basis. However, such an approach would miss the point, and not only because I seriously doubt that the statistical elegance of a general linear regression model is attainable. More fundamentally, the intricacy of multiple causal relationships, let alone of feedback loops further driving the system into one or several directions, rather indicates that the essence of the Bell Beaker Phenomenon is its emergence (Figure 20). By emergence, I specifically refer to a property often encapsulated by the old adage that 'the whole is more than the sum of its parts'.

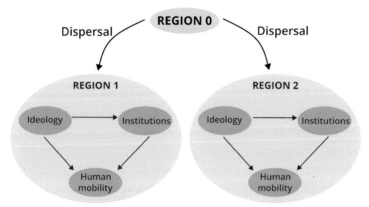

Stage 1: initial dispersal and regional variation

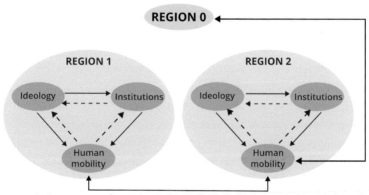

Stage 2: increased regional variation through local feedback loops and inter-group interaction

Figure 20 Schematic explanation of the Bell Beaker Phenomenon as a complex system. During Stage 1, an initial dispersal leads to a series of regional variants of the original system. In Stage 2, feedback loops between components of individual systems, and intergroup interactions increase in a nonlinear way the overall level of regional variation, possibly leading to further episodes of dispersal.

In complex systems theory, an emergent property is generally defined as a feature of a system which is not present in any of its individual components, and which cannot be directly derived from the rules dictating their individual interactions. The biologist Peter Corning (2002: 22) considers that an emerging property must fulfil five key criteria, largely paraphrased here:

(1) it must be radically novel (i.e., not previously seen in the system);
(2) it presents a level of coherence (i.e., the integrated whole will have some temporal duration);
(3) it happens at a global or macro 'level';
(4) it is the outcome of a dynamic process; and
(5) it is 'ostensive', in the sense that it can be observed, more generally in the form of a pattern.

Let us consider each of these points, though not in the original sequential order. The oft-quoted radical novelty is perhaps the less contentious, and the preceding pages have made clear that, while individual mechanisms comparable to those observed in the Bell Beaker Phenomenon can be found in some regions in the preceding centuries, their scale and combination during the second half of the 3rd millennium calBC are unmatched for the entirety of later European Prehistory.

Corning's final point on the 'ostensive' character of emergence strongly resonates with the repeated argument that the central issue with the Bell Beaker Phenomenon lies in the description of its variations, and thus the elucidation of regional and supra-regional patterns. Points 2 and 3 are analytical extensions of this pattern-oriented search, through the characterisation of metapopulation as a key property of integration and wholeness of the period. Point 4 insists on the dynamical dimension of connectivity as an emergent property. Following the lead of many others, I have stressed how much the Bell Beaker Phenomenon as a global process is a comparatively short-lived event spanning two to three centuries at most and then followed by increased regionalism in the form of local groups with Beaker typological roots of various kinds. This two-stage sequence is best articulated by Stuart Needham's contrast between his fusion and fission horizons to account for the changing relationships across Britain and north-western continental Europe (Needham 2005). While at least in typological terms the high level of interaction is of short duration, it is noteworthy that the flow of people, in many forms, extends well beyond this stage. In this sense, there is no contradiction between the fact that, on the one hand, the individual trajectory of each local group appears largely independent (i.e., characterised by its own typological development) and, on the other hand, that the whole structure, as a metapopulation, remains unchanged and provides an overarching framework for the movement of people.

5 A Few Points to Conclude

In the introduction we asked a seemingly simple yet challenging question: Is the concept of an archaeological culture still relevant? This question is perhaps not as remedial as it may at first seem, as recent technical advances have led to the resurrection of migratory narratives which seem directly lifted from culture-historical textbooks. My argument is that the return of migrations demands a reconsideration of archaeological cultures because of the need to challenge the worrying naivety attached to such interpretations, and because the discipline has come full circle since the concept was first defined. Just as archaeological cultures grew out of the need to account for more data, the present-day empirical diversity requires integrative, synthetic concepts. Theoretical and methodological cohesiveness can arguably be sought within and outside our discipline, but seeking solace in archaeological cultures makes sense as they require direct engagement with the complexity of data, and the multiplicity of scales and signals they potentially encompass.

To this end, the bulk of this element aimed to offer a brief overview of the available evidence, and, more fundamentally, to stress how much the description per se of the Bell Beaker variation is an interpretative act. In this it differs from many older studies which were restricted to a few selected tropes. What emerges from this exercise is that the Bell Beaker Phenomenon can advantageously be described as an archaeological culture at two congruent levels since, either at the level of the discontinuous patch or at the level of the whole BBP, the archaeological record presents an undeniable degree of structured variation, and thus a narrow definition as a mere list of given material types remains out of reach and illusory. As discussed in the preceding section, the key lies in identifying a mechanism which allows us to resolve both scales at once. This is a condition that is met by the idea of the Bell Beaker Phenomenon as an emergent metapopulation. This final suggestion is likely to feel somewhat tentative to many readers, partly due to the difficulties inherent in assessing archaeological evidence through the lens of theoretical ecology.

Salvation does not lie in a purely theoretical discourse. Aside from the fact that the metapopulation model echoes existing notions of migration and mobility, the rationale for such an abstract theoretical concept is that apart from dealing with the oft-acknowledged Bell Beaker uniqueness, it offers alternative interpretative directions. In this sense, for the concept to be truly successful, one would need to test it formally and demonstrate how the requirements of such test would open new avenues for research. Such an enterprise would be articulated along two axes: firstly, anchoring with greater accuracy and precision the spatial limits and idiosyncrasies of individual patches; secondly, a renewed characterisation and measure of human connectivity. The rest of this conclusion briefly explores the implications of this focus on metapopulation for gathering and interrogating present and future data, for revisiting and detoxifying older interpretative themes, and for overhauling the seemingly never-ending quest for 'the explanation' of the Bell Beaker Phenomenon.

5.1 Data, Data, Data

Having reached the final stage of this short journey across the Bell Beaker Phenomenon, it is traditional, if not compulsory, to consider the imperious need to obtain more data, and to list the particular domains where the dearth of such evidence is most obvious. Assuredly, from the point of view of improved patch characterisation, further settlement data would be welcome, and one can expect more information to become available under the impetus of landscape-scaled projects only possible with the financial and logistic means of development-led archaeology. Such sites would in turn allow us to acquire much needed zooarchaeological and archaeobotanical data to get the pulse of Bell Beaker subsistence economy, an area where high variation is expected in view of the latitudinal spread of the phenomenon. Likewise, considering the question of connectivity, improved ancient DNA coverage would feature at the top of any data wish list, and, in the few years since the publication of Olalde et al.'s (2018) seminal paper, regional transects and methodological innovations have already given us a glimpse of future gains to come. Such empirical imperatives are without doubt essential although, to be honest, such a statement amounts to little more than a cliché.

Indeed, a bigger challenge lies ahead in terms of collecting, analysing, and sharing old and future data. Open science, FAIR and CARE principles, and 'big data' have over the past few years slowly morphed from buzzwords to emerging realities and calls for best practices in archaeology. The picture, however, changes between regional research traditions and fields of expertise, and personal experience suggests that, most unfortunately, Bell Beaker studies lag some way behind in this process. For instance, the mapping provided in Figure 1 was unachievable until the completion of Bilger's thesis (Bilger 2019), although access to the data itself was kindly provided by the author. Indeed, while the idea of a Bell Beaker atlas or pan-regional catalogue has been floated on several occasions at conferences I had the opportunity to attend, it has failed to materialise for various reasons, though regional exceptions are noticeable and laudable (e.g., Kolar et al. 2022). Likewise, radiocarbon datasets have flourished over the past decade but offer at best a starting point for further work rather than a coherent resource. Ancient DNA sequences are, by contrast, made available immediately at time of publication via dedicated repositories, and updated lists are managed by individual laboratories, though unstructured archaeological labelling of samples is noticeable and hampers ready reuse by non-specialists. Isotopic data are also often published in the form of supplementary information and several initiatives have been put forward to centralise records though, to my knowledge, none can pretend to be exhaustive, and a period-specific Bell Beaker compilation remains lacking. Arguably, the situation is not eased by the geographical span of the Bell Beaker Phenomenon, but this short list highlights how much the creation of any dataset can prove a Sisyphean task. In this sense, the acquisition of new data, including through new sampling and excavation, requires a fundamental overhaul that depends first and foremost on how we consider and treat information.

5.2 Detoxifying Interpretative Themes

The absence of readily available synthetic datasets, in contrast to data in the form of papers and monographs, is detrimental to the production of knowledge, a situation even more damaging in view of the popular interest triggered by the Bell Beaker Phenomenon. Under the impetus of ancient DNA findings, the Bell Beaker Phenomenon has experienced a renewed interest in popular outlets and online forums, a trajectory which poses many problems. It is hard to deny that gender identity constitutes a recurring structuring dimension of Bell Beaker funerary practices. Yet, as ever with the Bell Beaker period, any closer examination reveals a kaleidoscope of regional variations and the existence of numerous exceptions, thus challenging the identification of any straightforward pattern. In a related way, much has recently been written on post-marital exchange rules, with a strong tendency to identify women as passive actors being relocated between villages. Here also, empirical evidence paints a more diverse picture than is sometimes acknowledged. In both cases, stressing variation is essential to counteract uncritical projections of contemporary gender relations and expected roles (Frieman et al. 2019). Likewise, the return of migration towards the top of the agenda has been accompanied by increased references to the Bell Beaker Phenomenon in varied media, including those expressing nationalistic and far-right views. Others have commented upon this worrying trend much better than me, but the key argument is worth repeating here: through an active and explicit politics of public engagement, some of the

leading aDNA laboratories, as well as some of their key archaeological collaborators, have actively promoted and disseminated interpretations set in simplistic terms, thus facilitating their re-appropriation by extreme groups (Hakenbeck
2019). Here as well, increased interpretative sophistication and theoretical
imagination are required to counter-balance the toxic potential inherent in
simple, attractive, and easily marketable narratives.

The key message is that such complexity must be supported, substantiated, and
accompanied by an active involvement in data management and sharing. The
implied shift in attitude is even more imperative as archaeologists are increasingly
required to manipulate and evaluate an ever-growing diversity of strands of
evidence on a daily basis. Kristian Kristiansen recently suggested that the value
of new 'scientific' data rests in their capacity to provide intellectual freedom
(Kristiansen 2022). I would rather suggest that intellectual freedom was and is
always present, and that data, novel in their scope as they might be, ought never to
drive the agenda which, under these conditions, can only be reactive and oppor-
tunistic at best. Any intellectual source of inspiration – anthropological, philo-
sophical, ecological – is welcome, as long as it opens new paths allowing for the
exploration of new territories. From this perspective, the idea set forth here of the
Bell Beaker Phenomenon as an emergent metapopulation presents at least two
advantages. Firstly, it offers a radical departure from the unimaginative previous
tropes which litter the Bell Beaker historiography; secondly, it allows us to
reconsider in a new light the twin question of is the nature of the Bell Beaker
Phenomenon and how it differs from previous periods.

5.3 How Rather Than Why

Evidential problems such as those mentioned above are detrimental in several
ways. For instance, to go back to metapopulation and emergence, a massive
part of the appeal of using such concepts and the fields associated with them
lies in the available array of formal statistical and computational models that
accompany them. Such models provide ways to translate the multiplicity of
corresponding data into rules and thus to move away from simple causal
models (i.e., stressing the role of a single factor) towards the identification
of emergent properties, the creation of feedback loops between different
mechanisms, and other processes explored by complex systems theory (e.g.,
Levin 1999). While such models can be built from theoretical first principles
only, an extensive literature demonstrates how such conceptual exercises can
also be driven by data exploration (so-called pattern-oriented modelling:
Grimm et al. 2005). Metapopulation properties can be tested by incorporating
information on the ecological make-up and spatial structure of patches, their

carrying capacity, and estimates of population size and connectivity (e.g., proportion of individuals moving from patch to patch) (Sample et al. 2018). Translated into archaeological terms, it is unlikely that precise values can be inferred from the available data alone, though reducing the range of the parameters by reference to data would already be a huge pioneering undertaking. Rather than co-opting ecological models in an uncritical fashion, the real challenge thus lies in creating new, more appropriate models, informed by systematic and synthetic account of the data, rather than mere 'hunches' as is the case here. Last but not least, cohesive datasets would also play an essential role in testing the simulated outputs and predictions of these computational models. All in all, such data and subsequent analysis would make it possible to better delineate and characterise the individual patches in Figure 21, as well as to identify and weigh the properties of the links between them, rather than the generalized arrows suggesting the directional flows of influence as is still necessary now.

Figure 21 Bell Beaker phenomenon as a metapopulation.

If the metapopulation model provides an accurate description and explanation for the Bell Beaker Phenomenon, one can reasonably expect some level of predictability in the data and thus in the generation of hypotheses to be tested. The central tenet of the concept is that, though the trajectory of each patch remains largely independent and thus prone to stochasticity, the overall structure remains stable over the long term. As we have seen, this property echoes the fact that each Bell Beaker region presents its own undeniable identity and that it is hard to eschew the reality of the wholeness of the Bell Beaker Phenomenon. To echo the subtitle of this Element, we are witnessing a harmony of difference. But we can perhaps go one step further. In the original model, the stochastic character of each patch implies continuous fluctuations, sometimes leading to local cycles of extinction and repopulation. Although nothing so dramatic occurs in the archaeological record of the 3rd millennium calBC, this raises the question of whether or not such local demographic oscillations actually happened, and if their potential negative impact was negated through the extensive connectivity underlying the overall network. The identification of such a double mechanism requires a careful multi-proxy appraisal of the fine-grained demographic history of individual patches (e.g., population size and demographic structure) and a high-resolution chronology to identify temporal relationships between them. Although such requirements are not strictly met right now, I would suggest that such model could account for the apparent synchrony between the fission horizon in many parts of north-western Europe, and the northward expansion of Bell Beaker traits and farming in northern parts of Scandinavia.

Regardless of the future success or failure of this last hypothesis, this example has attempted to showcase the merits of recasting older questions within a renewed conceptual framework. While I am not so pretentious as to seek to recommend any particular path beyond my own theoretical inclinations, I am tempted to say that some of the points made here probably have wider relevance for the discipline. Debates on the role of 'archaeological science', itself an unsatisfactory umbrella term for a huge range of analytical techniques and methods, raged in the early 2000s and never entirely faltered as indicated by some early reactions to ancient DNA studies. Yet, the discipline has moved on towards a more realistic position and the use of such methods is unlikely to diminish, instead becoming routine. If the archaeological toolbox is possibly one of the most varied ones around, such multiplicity and the technical approaches that support it can be daunting to say the least, and demand equally systematic action in terms of data management and conceptual imagination.

Metapopulation's defining characteristic is connectivity, as it is what makes the whole more than the sum of its parts. Connectivity is a trait of many human societies and can be identified across later European prehistory through multiple methods and proxies. However, in the case of the Bell Beaker Phenomenon, connectivity, especially the structured flow of individuals between patches, undergoes a qualitative shift and becomes the defining feature of the system. Obviously, the Bell Beaker Phenomenon is more than mobility, and the role of other factors in propping up this structure has to be re-evaluated. But such investigation, in contrast to over a century of research into this topic, will require explicit consideration of multiple factors, and concepts such as multi-scalar, non-linearity, feedback loops, or cascade effects, to name but a few. A future framed in such a way may sound strange, less familiar than one built on old comfortable themes, and thus unsettling, but is and will prove exciting, promising, and ultimately rewarding.

References

Abercromby, J. 1902. The oldest Bronze-Age ceramic type in Britain; its close analogies on the Rhine; its probable origins in central Europe. *The Journal of the Anthropological Institute of Great Britain and Ireland* 32: 373–397. https://doi.org/10.2307/2842826.

Allentoft, M. E., Sikora, M., Sjögren, K. -G. et al. 2015. Population genomics of Bronze Age Eurasia. *Nature* 522(7555): 167–172. https://doi.org/10.1038/nature14507.

Allentoft, M. E., Sikora, M., Refoyo-Martinez, A. et al. 2024: Population genomics of Stone Age Eurasia. *Nature*, 625(7994), 329–337. https://doi.org/10.1038/s41586-023-06862-3.

Ambert, P., and Carozza, L. 1996. Origine et développement de la première métallurgie française: état de la question. *Archéologie en Languedoc* 20: 43–56.

Aranda Jiménez, G., Milesi García, L., Hamilton, D. et al. 2022. The tempo of the Iberian megalithic rituals in the European context: The cemetery of Panoría. *Journal of Archaeological Science* 140: 105579. https://doi.org/10.1016/j.jas.2022.105579.

Armit, I., and Reich, D. 2021. The return of the Beaker folk? Rethinking migration and population change in British prehistory. *Antiquity* 95: 1464–1477. https://doi.org/10.15184/aqy.2021.129.

Bailly, M. 2014. Discordance des temps, concordance des espaces? Remarques sur les armatures de flèches en contexte campaniforme de l'arc jurassien à l'isthme européen. In Arbogast R.-M., and Greffier-Richard A., eds., *Entre archéologie et écologie, une Préhistoire de tous les milieux: Mélanges offerts à Pierre Pétrequin*. Besançon: Presses universitaires de Franche-Comté: 355–386.

Baioni, M., Martini, F., Nicolis, F., Poggiani Keller, R., and Sarti, L. 2019. Bell Beaker settlements in northern and central Italy. In Gibson, A., ed., *The Bell Beaker settlement of Europe: The Bell Beaker Phenomenon from a domestic perspective*. Oxford: Oxbow Books: 131–149.

Banks, W.E., Antunes, N., Rigaud, S., and d'Errico, F. 2013. Ecological constraints on the first prehistoric farmers in Europe. *Journal of Archaeological Science* 40(6): 2746–2753. https://doi.org/10.1016/j.jas.2013.02.013.

Barge, H. 1982. *Les parures du Néolithique ancien au début de l'Age des Métaux en Languedoc*. Paris: CNRS.

Bayliss, A., Mc Avoy, F., and Whittle, A. 2007. The world recreated: Redating Silbury Hill in its monumental landscape. *Antiquity* 81: 26–53.

Beckerman, S. M. 2011–2. Dutch Beaker chronology re-examined. *Palaeohistoria* 53/54: 1–24. https://ugp.rug.nl/Palaeohistoria/article/view/24978.

Bentley, R. A. 2006. Strontium isotopes from the Earth to the archaeological skeleton: A review. *Journal of Archaeological Method and Theory* 13(3): 135–187. https://doi.org/10.1007/s10816-006-9009-x.

Besse, M. 2003. Les céramiques communes des Campaniformes européens. *Gallia Préhistoire* 45: 205–58. https://doi.org/10.3406/galip.2003.2039.

Bilger, M. 2019. Der Glockenbecher in Europa – eine Kartierung. *Journal of Neolithic Archaeology* 20: 203–270. https://doi.org/10.12766/jna.2018S.11.

Billard, C., Querré, G., and Salanova, L. 1998. Le phénomène campaniforme dans la basse vallée de la Seine: chronologie et relation habitats-sépultures. *Bulletin de la Société Préhistorique Française* 95: 351–64. https://doi.org/10.3406/bspf.1998.10810.

Billard, C. 2011. Les sépultures individuelles campaniformes de Normandie. In Salanova, L., and Tchérémissinoff, Y., eds., *Les sépultures individuelles campaniformes en Franc*. Paris: CNRS. Éditions: 37–45. https://doi.org/10.4000/books.editionscnrs.55000.

Bini, M., Zanchetta, G., Perşoiu, A. et al. 2019. The 4.2 ka BP event in the Mediterranean region: An overview. *Proxy Use-Development-Validation/Terrestrial Archives/Holocene* 2: 555–577. https://doi.org/10.5194/cp-2018-147-RC1.

Bishop, R. R. 2015. Did Late Neolithic farming fail or flourish? A Scottish perspective on the evidence for Late Neolithic arable cultivation in the British Isles. *World Archaeology* 47(5): 834–855. https://doi.org/10.1080/00438243.2015.1072477.

Blanco-González, A., Lillios, K. T., López-Sáez, J. A., and Drake, B. L. 2018. Cultural, demographic and environmental dynamics of the Copper and Early Bronze Age in Iberia (3300–1500 BC): Towards an interregional multiproxy comparison at the time of the 4.2 ky BP event. *Journal of World Prehistory* 31 (1): 1–79. https://doi.org/10.1007/s10963-018-9113-3.

Bloxam, A., and Pearson, M. P. 2022. Funerary diversity and cultural continuity: The British Beaker phenomenon beyond the stereotype. *Proceedings of the Prehistoric Society* 88: 261–284. https://doi.org/10.1017/ppr.2022.2.

Booth, T.J., Brück, J., Brace, S., and Barnes, I. 2021. Tales from the supplementary information: Ancestry change in Chalcolithic–Early Bronze Age Britain was gradual with varied kinship organization. *Cambridge Archaeological Journal* 31: 379–400. https://doi.org/10.1017/S0959774321000019.

Bourgeois, Q. 2013. *Monuments on the horizon: The formation of the Barrow Landscape throughout the 3nd and 2nd Millennium BCE*. Leiden: Sidestone Press.

Bourgeois, Q., Amkreutz, L., and Panhuysen, R. 2009. The Niersen Beaker burial: A renewed study of a century-old excavation. *Journal of Archaeology in the Low Countries* 1(2): 83–105. https://jalc.nl/cgi/t/text/get-pdfa2cd.pdf?c=jalc;idno=0102a04.

Bourgeois, Q., and Kroon, E. 2017. The impact of male burials on the construction of Corded Ware identity: Reconstructing networks of information in the 3rd millennium BC. *PloS One* 12(10): e0185971. https://doi.org/10.1371/journal.pone.0185971.

Bradley, R. 2019. *The Prehistory of Britain and Ireland*. Cambridge University Press. https://doi.org/10.1017/9781108419925.

Bradley, R., Haselgrove, C., Vander Linden, M., and Webley, L. 2016. *The Later Prehistory of North-West Europe: The Evidence of Development-Led Fieldwork*. Oxford: Oxford University Press.

Bradley, R. S., and Bakke, J. 2019. Is there evidence for a 4.2 ka BP event in the northern North Atlantic region? *Climate of the Past* 15(5): 1665–1676. https://doi.org/10.5194/cp-15-1665-2019.

Brandt, G., Haak, W., Adler, C. J. et al. 2013. Ancient DNA reveals key stages in the formation of central European mitochondrial genetic diversity. *Science* 342: 257–261. https://doi.org/10.1126/science.1241844.

Bray, P. J., and Pollard, A. M. 2012. A new interpretative approach to the chemistry of copper-alloy objects: Source, recycling and technology. *Antiquity* 86: 853–867. https://doi.org/10.1017/s0003598x00047967.

Britton, K., Crowley, B. E., Bataille, C. P., Miller, J. H., and Wooler, M. J. 2021. Silver linings at the dawn of a 'Golden Age'. *Frontiers in Ecology and Evolution* 9. https://doi.org/10.3389/fevo.2021.748938.

Brodie, N. 1994. *The Neolithic-Bronze Age Transition in Britain: A Critical Review of Some Archaeological and Craniological Concepts, British Archaeological Reports (British Series), 238*. Oxford: Archaeopress.

Brodie, N. 1997. New perspectives on the bell-beaker culture. *Oxford Journal of Archaeology* 16: 297–314. https://doi.org/10.1111/1468-0092.00042.

Bronk Ramsey, C. 2017. Methods for summarizing radiocarbon datasets. *Radiocarbon* 59: 1809–1833. https://doi.org/10.1017/RDC.2017.108.

Brotherton, P., Haak, W., Templeton, J. et al. 2013. Neolithic mitochondrial haplogroup H genomes and the genetic origins of Europeans. *Nature Communications* 4: 1764. https://doi.org/10.1038/ncomms2656.

Brunel, S., Bennett, E. A., Cardin, L. et al. 2020. Ancient genomes from present-day France unveil 7,000 years of its demographic history. *PNAS* 117: 12791–12798. . https://doi.org/10.1073/pnas.1918034117.

Brunner, M., von Felten, J., Hinz, M., and Hafner, A, 2020. Central European Early Bronze Age chronology revisited: A Bayesian examination of large-scale radiocarbon dating. *PloS One* 15: e0243719. https://doi.org/10 .1371/journal.pone.0243719.

Bueno Ramirez, P., Barroso Bermejo, R., and De Balbin Behrmann, R. 2005. Mégalithes dans le centre de la Péninsule ibérique: une perspective d'analyse à partir de la Meseta sud. In Joussaume, R., Laporte, L., and Scarre, C., eds., *Origin and Development of the Megalithic Phenomenon of Western Europe: Proceedings of the International Symposium (Bougon, France, October 26th-30th 2002)*. Niort: Conseil Général des Deux-Sèvres: 425–440.

Caraglio, A. 2020. How to redraw Bell Beaker networks in Southwestern Europe? *Préhistoires Méditerranéennes* 8. https://doi.org/10.4000/pm.2282.

Cardoso, J. L. 2014. Cronología absoluta del fenómeno campaniforme al Norte del estuario del Tajo: implicaciones demográficas y sociales. *Trabajos de Prehistoria* 71: 56–75. https://doi.org/10.3989/tp.2014.12124.

Carlin, N. 2018. *The Beaker Phenomenon? Understanding the Character and Context of Social Practices in Ireland 2500-2000 BC*. Leiden: Sidestone Press.

Carloni, D., Šegvić, B., Sartoi, M., Zanoni, G., and Besse, M. 2023. Who venerated the ancestors at the Petit-Chasseur site? Examining Early Bronze Age cultic activities around megalithic monuments through the archaeometric analyses of ceramic findings (Upper Rhône Valley, Switzerland, 2200-1600 BC). *Archaeological and Anthropological Sciences* 15(5): 62. https://doi.org/10.1007/s12520-023-01737-0.

Cassidy, L. M., Martiniano, R., Murphy, E. M. et al. 2016. Neolithic and Bronze Age migration to Ireland and establishment of the insular Atlantic genome. *PNAS* 113: 368–373. https://doi.org/10.1073/pnas.1518445113.

Cauliez, J. 2011. Restitution des aires culturelles au Néolithique final dans le sud-est de la France. Dynamiques de formation et d'évolution des styles céramiques. *Gallia préhistoire* 53: 85–202. https://doi.org/10.3406/galip.2011.2488.

Childe, V. G. 1957. *The Dawn of European Civilization*. London: Routledge & Kegan Paul Ltd.

Clark, G. 1966. The invasion hypothesis in British archaeology. *Antiquity* 40: 172–189. https://doi.org/10.1017/S0003598X00032488.

Clarke, D. L. 1968. *Analytical Archaeology*. London: Routledge.

Clarke, D. L. 1970. *Beaker Pottery of Great Britain and Ireland*. Cambridge: Cambridge University Press.

Clarke, D. L. 1976. The Beaker network – social and economic models. In Lanting, J. N., and van der Waals, J. D., eds., *Glockenbecher Symposion Oberried (1974)*. Haarlem: Fibula–Van Dishoeck: 459–477.

Collar, A., Coward, F., Brughmans, T., and Mills, B. J. 2015. Networks in archaeology: Phenomena, abstraction, representation. *Journal of Archaeological Method and Theory* 22: 1–32. https://doi.org/10.1007/s10816-014-9235-6.

Corning, P. A. 2002. The re-emergence of 'emergence': A venerable concept in search of a theory. *Complexity* 7: 18–30. https://doi.org/10.1002/cplx.10043.

Courtin, J., Bouville, C., Lemercier, O. et al. 2011. La sépulture campaniforme d'enfant de la Grotte Murée, Montagnac-Montpezat (Alpes-de-Haute-Provence). In Salanova, L., and Tchérémissinoff, Y., eds., *Les sépultures individuelles campaniformes en France*. Paris: CNRS Éditions: 161–166. https://doi.org/10.4000/books.editionscnrs.55145.

Czebreszuk, J., ed., 2014. *Similar but Different: Bell Beakers in Europe*. Leiden: Sidestone Press.

Czebreszuk, J., and Szmyt, M. 2019. Bell Beaker domestic sites and houses in the Polish lands: Odra and Visutal catchments. In Gibson, A., ed., *The Bell Beaker Settlement of Europe: The Bell Beaker Phenomenon from a Domestic Perspective*. Oxford: Oxbow Books: 255–275.

Darvill, T., Marshall, P., Parker Pearson, M., and Wainwright, G 2009. Stonehenge remodelled. *Antiquity* 86: 1021–1040. https://doi.org/10.1017/S0003598X00048225.

de Jesus Sanches, M., and Barbosa, H. 2018. Campaniforme: A long term phenomenon in the Portuguese Douro basin. *Journal of Neolithic Archaeology* 4: 23–58. https://doi.org/10.12766/jna.2018S.3.

de Vries, H., Barendsen, G. W., and Waterbolk, H. T. 1958. Groningen radiocarbon dates II. *Science* 127: 129–137. https://doi.org/10.1126/science.127.3290.129.

Dias, M. I., Prudêncio, M. I., and Valera, A. C. 2017. Provenance and circulation of Bell Beakers from Western European societies of the 3rd millennium BC: The contribution of clays and pottery analyses. *Applied Clay Science* 146: 334–342. https://doi.org/10.1016/j.clay.2017.06.026.

Díaz-del-Río, P., Uriarte, A., Becerra, P., Pérez-Villa, A., Vicent, J. M., and Díaz-Zorita, M. 2022. Paleomobility in Iberia: 12 years of strontium isotope research. *Journal of Archaeological Science Reports* 46: 103653. https://doi.org/10.1016/j.jasrep.2022.103653.

Díaz-Zorita Bonilla, M., Beck, J., Bocherens, H. et al. 2018. Isotopic evidence for mobility at large-scale human aggregations in Copper Age Iberia: The mega-site of Marroquíes. *Antiquity* 92: 991–1007. https://doi.org/10.15184/aqy.2018.33.

Dolfini, A. 2014. Early metallurgy in the central Mediterranean. In Roberts, B. W., and Thornton, C. P., eds., *Archaeometallurgy in Global Perspective:*

Methods and Syntheses. New York: Springer: 473–506. https://doi.org/10.1007/978-1-4614-9017-3_18.

Dolfini, A. 2019. From the Neolithic to the Bronze Age in Central Italy: Settlement, burial, and social change at the dawn of metal production. *Journal of Archaeological Research* 28: 503–556. https://doi.org/10.1007/s10814-019-09141-w.

Dolfini, A. 2022. Warrior graves reconsidered: Metal, power and identity in Copper Age Italy. *World Archaeology* 53: 809–833. https://doi.org/10.1080/00438243.2021.2013307.

Dorado Alejos, A., Mederos Martín, A., González Quintero, P. et al. 2021. The ceramic productions of Puente de Santa Bárbara: A Bell Beaker metallurgical centre in the Almanzora Basin (Huércal-Overa, Almería, SE Spain). *Archaeological and Anthropological Sciences* 13: 82. https://doi.org/10.1007/s12520-021-01316-1.

Drenth, E., Freudenberg, M., and Williams, G. 2016. The belongings of a Bell Beaker smith? A stone hoard from Hengelo, province of Gelderland, the Netherlands. *Musaica Archaeologica* 1: 37–58.

Dulias, K., Foody, M. G. B., Justeau, P. et al. 2022. Ancient DNA at the edge of the world: Continental immigration and the persistence of Neolithic male lineages in Bronze Age Orkney. *PNAS* 119: e2108001119. https://doi.org/10.1073/pnas.2108001119.

Egfjord, A. F.-H., Margaryan, A., Fischer, A. et al. 2021. Genomic steppe ancestry in skeletons from the Neolithic single grave culture in Denmark. *PloS One* 16: e0244872. https://doi.org/10.1371/journal.pone.0244872.

Evans, J. A., Chenery, C. A., and Fitzpatrick, A. P. 2006. Bronze Age childhood migration of individuals near Stonehenge revealed by strontium and oxygen isotope tooth enamel analysis. *Archaeometry* 48: 309–321. https://doi.org/10.1111/j.1475-4754.2006.00258.x.

Favrel, Q., and Nicolas, C. 2022. Bell Beaker burial customs in North-western France. *Proceedings of the Prehistoric Society* 88: 285–320. https://doi.org/10.1017/ppr.2022.13.

Fernandes, D. M., Mittnik, A., Olalde, I. et al. 2020. The spread of steppe and Iranian-related ancestry in the islands of the western Mediterranean. *Nature Ecology & Evolution* 4: 334–345. https://doi.org/10.1038/s41559-020-1102-0.

Fernández-Crespo, T., Ordoño, J., Barandiarán, I., Andrés, M. T., and Schulting, R. J. 2019. The Bell Beaker multiple burial pit of La Atalayuela (La Rioja, Spain): stable isotope insights into diet, identity and mortuary practices in Chalcolithic Iberia. *Archaeological and Anthropological Sciences* 11: 3733–3749. https://doi.org/10.1007/s12520-018-0610-1

Fitzpatrick, A. P. 2013. *The Amesbury Archer and the Boscombe Bowmen: Early Bell Beaker Burials at Boscombe Down, Amesbury, Wiltshire, Great Britain: Excavations at Boscombe Down, Volume 1*. Salisbury: Wessex Archaeology.

Fokkens, H., and Nicolis, F., eds., 2012. *Background to Beakers: Inquiries in Regional Cultural Backgrounds to the Bell Beaker Complex*. Leiden: Sidestone Press.

Fokkens, H., Achterkamp, Y., and Kuijpers, M. 2008. Bracers or bracelets? About the functionality and meaning of Bell Beaker wrist-guards. *Proceedings of the Prehistoric Society* 74: 79–108. https://doi.org/10.1017/S0079497X00000165.

Fokkens, H., Steffens, B. J. W., and van As, S. F. M. 2016. *Farmers, Fishers, Fowlers, Hunters: Knowledge Generated by Development-Led Archaeology about the Late Neolithic, the Early Bronze Age and the Start of the Middle Bronze Age (2850-1500 cal BC) in the Netherlands*. Amersfoort: Rijksdienst voor het Cultureel Erfgoed.

Frei, K. M., Bergerbant, S., Sjögren, K. - G. et al. 2019. Mapping human mobility during the third and second millennia BC in present-day Denmark. *PloS One* 14: e0219850. https://doi.org/10.1371/journal.pone.0219850.

Frieman, C. J., Teather, A., and Morgan, C. 2019. Bodies in motion: Narratives and counter narratives of gendered mobility in European later prehistory. *Norwegian Archaeological Review* 52: 148–169. https://doi.org/10.1080/00293652.2019.1697355.

Furestier, R. 2007. *Les industries lithiques campaniformes du sud-est de la France*. British Archaeological Reports International Series 1684. Oxford: Archaeopress.

Furholt, M. 2014. Upending a 'Totality': Re-evaluating Corded Ware variability in Late Neolithic Europe. *Proceedings of the Prehistoric Society* 80: 67–86. https://doi.org/10.1017/ppr.2013.20.

Furholt, M. 2018. Massive Migrations? The impact of recent aDNA studies on our view of third millennium Europe. *European Journal of Archaeology* 21: 159–191. https://doi.org/10.1017/eaa.2017.43.

Furholt, M. 2019. Re-integrating archaeology: A contribution to aDNA studies and the migration discourse on the 3rd millennium BC in Europe. *Proceedings of the Prehistoric Society* 85: 115–129. https://doi.org/10.1017/ppr.2019.4.

Gallay, A. 1973. Le phénomène campaniforme: une nouvelle hypothèse historique. *Archives suisses d'anthropologie générale* 43: 231–258.

Gandois, H., Burlot, A., Mille, B., and de Veslud C. 2019. Early Bronze Age axe-ingots from Brittany: Evidence for connections with south-west Ireland? *Proceedings of the Royal Irish Academy: Archaeology, Culture, History, Literature* 119C: 1–36. https://doi.org/10.3318/priac.2019.119.04.

Gandois, H., Rousseau, L., Gehres, B. et al. 2020. New hints of metallurgical activity on the Atlantic coast of France in the mid third millennium BC: Overview and perspectives on Beaker metallurgy in western Europe. *The Antiquaries Journal* 100: 1–32. https://doi.org/10.1017/S000358152 0000153.

García Sanjuán, L., Vargas Jiménez, J. M., Cáceres Puro, L. M. et al. 2018. Assembling the dead, gathering the living: Radiocarbon dating and Bayesian modelling for Copper Age Valencina de la Concepción (Seville, Spain). *Journal of World Prehistory* 31: 179–313. https://doi.org/10.1007/s10963-018-9114-2.

Garrido-Pena, R. 1997. Bell Beakers in the southern Meseta of the Iberian Peninsula: Socioeconomic context and new data. *Oxford Journal of Archaeology* 16: 187–209. https://doi.org/10.1111/1468-0092.00034.

Garrido-Pena, R. 2019. Living with Beakers in the interior of Iberia. In Gibson, A. ed., *The Bell Beaker Settlement of Europe: The Bell Beaker Phenomenon from a Domestic Perspective*. Oxford: Oxbow Books: 45–66.

Garrido-Pena, R., Flores Fernández, R., Herrero-Corral, A. M. et al. 2022. Atlantic halberds as Bell Beaker weapons in Iberia: Tomb 1 of Humanejos (Parla, Madrid, Spain). *Oxford Journal of Archaeology* 41: 252–277. https://doi.org/10.1111/ojoa.12250.

Gašpar, A., Petřík, A., Fotjík, P. et al. (2023). Beyond technology: Pottery reveals translocal social relations at a Bell Beaker monumental site in central Europe. *European Journal of Archaeology* 26: 299–319. https://doi.org/10.1017/eaa.2022.46.

Gibson, A., ed., 2019a. *The Bell Beaker Settlement of Europe: The Bell Beaker Phenomenon from a Domestic Perspective*. Oxford: Oxbow Books.

Gibson, A. 2019b. Beaker domestic architecture in Britain and Ireland. In Gibson, A., ed., *The Bell Beaker Settlement of Europe: The Bell Beaker Phenomenon from a Domestic Perspective*. Oxford: Oxbow Books: 309–328.

Goldberg, A., Günther, T., Rosenberg, N. A., and Jakobsson, M. 2017a. Ancient X chromosomes reveal contrasting sex bias in Neolithic and Bronze Age Eurasian migrations. *PNAS* 114: 2657–2662. https://doi.org/10.1073/pnas.1616392114.

Goldberg, A., Günther, T., Rosenberg, N. A., and Jakobsson, M. 2017b. Reply to Lazaridis and Reich: Robust model-based inference of male-biased admixture during Bronze Age migration from the Pontic-Caspian Steppe. *PNAS* 114: E3875–E3877. https://doi.org/10.1073/pnas.1704442114.

González-Fortes, G., Tassi, F., Trucchi, E. et al. 2019. A western route of prehistoric human migration from Africa into the Iberian Peninsula. *Proceedings of the Royal Society B: Biological Sciences* 286: 20182288. https://doi.org/10.1098/rspb.2018.2288.

Greaney, S., Hazell, Z., Barclay, A. et al. 2020. Tempo of a mega-henge: A new chronology for Mount Pleasant, Dorchester, Dorset. *Proceedings of the Prehistoric Society* 86: 199–236. https://doi.org/10.1017/ppr.2020.6.

Grimm, V., Revilla, E., Berger, U. et al. 2005. Pattern-oriented modeling of agent-based complex systems: Lessons from ecology. *Science* 310: 987–991. https://doi.org/10.1126/science.1116681.

Guilaine, J., and Zammit, J. 2001. *Le sentier de la guerre: visages de la violence préhistorique*. Paris: Seuil.

Haak, W., Lazaridis, I., Patterson, N. et al. 2015. Massive migration from the steppe was a source for Indo-European languages in Europe. *Nature* 522: 207–211. https://doi.org/10.1038/nature14317.

Hakenbeck, S. E. 2019. Genetics, archaeology and the far right: An unholy Trinity. *World Archaeology* 51: 517–527. https://doi.org/10.1080/00438243.2019.1617189.

Hanski, I., and Ovaskainen, O. 2003. Metapopulation theory for fragmented landscapes. *Theoretical Population Biology* 64: 119–127. https://doi.org/10.1016/S0040-5809(03)00022-4.

Harrison, R. 1980. *The Beaker Folk*. London: Thames & Hudson.

Harrison, R., and Heyd, V. 2007. The transformation of Europe in the third millennium BC: The example of 'Le Petit-Chasseur I + III' (Sion, Valais, Switzerland). *Praehistorische Zeitschrift* 82: 129–214. https://doi.org/10.1515/PZ.2007.010.

Herrero-Corral, A. M., Garrido-Pena, R., and Flores Fernández, R. 2019. The inheritors: Bell Beaker children's tombs in Iberia and their social context (2500–2000 CalBC). *Journal of Mediterranean Archaeology* 32: 63–87. https://doi.org/10.1558/jma.39328.

Ihuel, E. 2014. *La diffusion du silex du Grand-Pressigny dans le massif Armoricain au Néolithique*. Paris: C.T.H.S.

James, H. F., Willmes, M., Boel, C. A. et al. 2019. Who's been using my burial mound? Radiocarbon dating and isotopic tracing of human diet and mobility at the collective burial site, Le Tumulus des Sables, southwest France. *Journal of Archaeological Science: Reports* 24: 955–966. https://doi.org/10.1016/j.jasrep.2019.03.012.

Jeunesse, C. 2015. The dogma of the Iberian origin of the Bell Beaker: Attempting its deconstruction. *Journal of Neolithic Archaeology*: 158–166. https://doi.org/10.12766/jna.2014.5.

Joseph, F., Julien, M., Leroy-Langelin, E., Lorin, Y., and Praud, I. 2011. L'architecture domestique des sites du 3e millénaire avant notre ère dans le Nord de la France. *Revue Archéoloqique de Picardie* 28: 249–273. https://doi.org/10.3406/pica.2011.3333.

Kern, D., Morschhauser, G., Penz, M., and Schmitsberger, O. 2019. Late Neolithic and Bell Beaker settlements in (eastern) Austria. In Gibson, A., ed., *The Bell Beaker Settlement of Europe: The Bell Beaker Phenomenon from a Domestic Perspective*. Oxford: Oxbow Books: 177–193.

Kinnes, I. A., Gibson, A. M., Ambers, J. et al. 1991. Radiocarbon dating and the British Beakers: The British museum programme. *Scottish Archaeological Review* 8: 35–68.

Kleijne, J. P. 2019. *Embracing Bell Beaker: Adopting New Ideas and Objects across Europe during the Later 3rd Millennium BC (c. 2600-2000BC)*. Leiden: Sidestone Press.

Kleijne, J. P. and Drenth, E. 2019. An overview of Bell Beaker house plans in the Netherlands. In Gibson, A., ed., *The Bell Beaker Settlement of Europe: The Bell Beaker Phenomenon from a Domestic Perspective*. Oxford: Oxbow Books: 295–308.

Knipper, C., Mittnik, A., Massy, K. et al. 2017. Female exogamy and gene pool diversification at the transition from the Final Neolithic to the Early Bronze Age in central Europe. *PNAS* 114: 10083–10088. https://doi.org/10.1073/pnas.1706355114.

Kolář, J., Macek, M., Tkáč, P., Novák, P., and Abraham, V. 2022. Long-term demographic trends and spatio-temporal distribution of past human activity in Central Europe: Comparison of archaeological and palaeoecological proxies. *Quaternary Science Reviews* 297: 107834. https://doi.org/10.1016/j.quascirev.2022.107834.

Kristiansen, K. 2022. Archaeology and the genetic revolution in European prehistory. *Elements in the Archaeology of Europe*. Cambridge: Cambridge University Press. https://doi.org/10.1017/9781009228701.

Kristiansen, K., Allentoft, M. E., Frei, K. M. et al. 2017. Re-theorising mobility and the formation of culture and language among the Corded Ware Culture in Europe. *Antiquity* 91: 334–347. https://doi.org/10.15184/aqy.2017.17.

Kroon, E. J., Huismans, D. J., Bourgeois, Q. P., Braekmans, D. J., and Fokkens, H. 2019. The introduction of Corded Ware Culture at a local level: An exploratory study of cultural change during the Late Neolithic of the Dutch West Coast through ceramic technology. *Journal of Archaeological Science: Reports* 26: 101873. https://doi.org/10.1016/j.jasrep.2019.101873.

Lanting, J. N., and van der Waals, J. D. 1976. Beaker culture relations in the Lower Rhine basin. In Lanting, J. N., and van der Waals J. D., eds., *Glockenbecher Symposion: Oberried (1974)*. Haarlem: Fibula–Van Dishoeck: 2–80.

Lazaridis, I., and Reich, D. 2017. Failure to replicate a genetic signal for sex bias in the steppe migration into central Europe. *PNAS* 114: E3873–E3874. https://doi.org/10.1073/pnas.1704308114.

Le Brun-Ricalens, F., Toussaint, M., and Valotteau, F. 2011. Les sépultures campaniformes d'Altwies – 'Op dem Boesch' (Grand-Duché de Luxembourg). In Salanova, L., and Tchérémissinoff, Y., eds., *Les sépultures individuelles campaniformes en France*. Paris: CNRS Éditions: 115–123. https://doi.org/10.4000/books.editionscnrs.55090.

Lechterbeck, J., Kerig, T., Kleinmann, A. et al. 2014. How was Bell Beaker economy related to Corded Ware and Early Bronze Age lifestyles? Archaeological, botanical and palynological evidence from the Hegau, Western Lake Constance region. *Environmental Archaeology* 19: 95–113. https://doi.org/10.1179/1749631413Y.0000000010.

Lefebvre, A., Gazenbeek, M., and Pernot, P. 2008. Les sépultures campaniformes du site de Mondelange 'La Sente' (Moselle). Résultats préliminaires. *Internéo* 7: 187–201.

Lefebvre, A., Franck, J., Veber, C., and Duval, H. 2011. Les sépultures individuelles campaniformes en Lorraine: l'exemple de Pouilly (Moselle) et d'Hatrize (Meurthe-et-Moselle). In Salanova, L., and Tchérémissinoff, Y., eds., *Les sépultures individuelles campaniformes en France*. Paris: CNRS Éditions: 97–113. https://doi.org/10.4000/books.editionscnrs.55065.

Lemercier, O. 2012. Interpreting the Beaker phenomenon in Mediterranean France: An Iron Age analogy. *Antiquity* 86: 131–143. https://doi.org/10.1017/s0003598x00062505.

Lemercier, O., Furestier, R., Müller, A. et al. 2011. La sépulture individuelle campaniforme de La Fare, Forcalquier (Alpes-de-Haute-Provence). In Salanova, L., and Tchérémissinoff, Y., eds., *Les sépultures individuelles campaniformes en France*. Paris: CNRS Éditions: 145–159. https://doi.org/10.4000/books.editionscnrs.55120.

Lemercier, O., and Tchérémissinoff, Y. 2011. Du Néolithique final au Bronze ancien: les sépultures individuelles campaniformes dans le sud de la France. In Salanova, L., and Tchérémissinoff, Y., eds., *Les sépultures individuelles campaniformes en France*. CNRS Éditions: 177–194. https://doi.org/10.4000/books.editionscnrs.55170.

Lemercier, O., Blaise, E., Convertini, F. et al. 2019. Beaker settlements in Mediterranean France in their cultural context. In Gibson, A., ed., *The Bell Beaker Settlement of Europe: The Bell Beaker Phenomenon from a Domestic perspective*. Oxford: Oxbow Books: 81–101.

Levin, S. 1999. *Fragile Dominion: Complexity and the Commons*. Cambridge, MA: Perseus.

Levins, R. 1969. Some demographic and genetic consequences of environmental heterogeneity for biological control. *Bulletin of the Entomological Society of America* 15: 237–240. https://doi.org/10.1093/besa/15.3.237.

Lévi-Strauss, C. 1949. *Les structures élémentaires de la parenté*. Paris: Presses Universitaires de France.

Lillios, K. T., Waterman, A. J., Artz, J. A., and Jospehs, R. L. 2010. The Neolithic-Early Bronze Age mortuary rockshelter of Bolores, Torres Vedras, Portugal. *Journal of Field Archaeology* 35: 19–39. https://doi.org/10.1179/009346910X12707320296630.

Lillios, K. T., Blanco-González, A., Drake, B. L., and Lóp-Sáez, J. A. 2016. Mid-late Holocene climate, demography, and cultural dynamics in Iberia: A multi-proxy approach. *Quaternary Science Reviews* 135: 138–153. https://doi.org/10.1016/j.quascirev.2016.01.011.

Lillios, K. T. 2020. Mobility and alterity in Iberian late prehistoric archaeology: Current research on the Neolithic–Early Bronze Age (6000–1500 BCE). *Annual Review of Anthropology* 49: 49–65. https://doi.org/10.1146/annurev-anthro-010220-042345.

Madgwick, R., Lamb, A. L., Sloane, H. et al. 2019. Multi-isotope analysis reveals that feasts in the Stonehenge environs and across Wessex drew people and animals from throughout Britain. *Science Advances* 5: eaau6078. https://doi.org/10.1126/sciadv.aau6078.

Marcigny, C., Carpentier, V., Ghesquière, E. et al. 2004. Sépultures de 'pêcheurs' de l'Âge du Bronze ancien à Bénouville 'les Hautes Coutures' (Calvados). *Bulletin de la Société préhistorique française* 101: 305–323. https://doi.org/10.3406/bspf.2004.12994.

Marcigny, C., and Ghesquière, E. 2003. Parcellaire et nécropoles de l'Âge du Bronze ancien à Bernières-sur-Mer (Calvados). *Bulletin de la Société préhistorique française* 100: 117–134. https://doi.org/10.3406/bspf.2003.12796.

Maréchal, D., Pétrequin, A. -M., Pétrequin, P., and Arbogast, R. - M. 1998. Les parures du Néolithique final à Chalain et Clairvaux. *Gallia Préhistoire* 40: 141–203. https://doi.org/10.3406/galip.1998.2397.

Martial, E., Médard, F., Cayol, N. et al. 2013. Chaîne opératoire textile au Néolithique final dans le nord de la France: méthodologie et premiers résultats de l'approche pluridisciplinaire. In Anderson, P. C., Cheval, C., and Durand, A., eds., *Regards croisés sur les outils liés au travail des végétaux. An interdisciplinary focus on plant-working tools. XXXIIIe rencontres internationales d'archéologie et d'histoire d'Antibes*. Antibes: APDCA: 341–354.

Melis, M. G. 2019. Bell Beaker evidence in the domestic sphere of island contexts: Sardinia and Sicily. In Gibson, A., ed., *The Bell Beaker Settlement of Europe: The Bell Beaker Phenomenon from a Domestic Perspective*. Oxford: Oxbow Books: 109–129.

Mittnik, A., Massy, K., Knipper, C. et al. 2019. Kinship-based social inequality in Bronze Age Europe. *Science* 366: 731–734. https://doi.org/10.1126/science.aax6219.

Monge Soares, A. M., Alves, L. C., Friade J. C. et al. 2012. Bell Beaker gold foils from Perdigões (Southern Portugal) – manufacture and use. *Proceedings of the 39th International Symposium for Archaeometry*: 120–124.

Montes-Landa, J., Murillo-Barroso, M., Montero-Ruiz, I., Rovira-Llorens, S., and Martinón-Torres, M. 2021. Interwoven traditions in Bell Beaker metallurgy: Approaching the social value of copper at Bauma del Serrat del Pont (Northeast Iberia). *PloS One* 16: e0255818. https://doi.org/10.1371/journal.pone.0255818.

Müller, A. 2001. Gender differentiation in burial rites and grave-goods in the Eastern or Bohemian-Moravian Group of the Bell Beaker Culture. In Nicolis, F., ed., *Bell Beakers Today: Pottery, People, Culture, Symbols in Prehistoric Europe*. Trento: Provincia Autonoma di Trento, Servizio Beni Culturali Ufficio Beni Archeologici: 589–599.

Müller, J., and van Willingen, S. 2001. New radiocarbon evidence for European Bell Beakers and the consequences for the diffusion of the Bell Beaker Phenomenon. In Nicolis, F., ed., *Bell Beakers Today: Pottery, People, Culture, Symbols in Prehistoric Europe*. Trento: Uffi cio Beni Archeologici: 59–80.

Murillo-Barroso, M., Martínon-Torres, M., Massieu, M. D. et al. 2017. Early metallurgy in SE Iberia. The workshop of Las Pilas (Mojácar, Almería, Spain). *Archaeological and Anthropological Sciences* 9: 1539–1569. https://doi.org/10.1007/s12520-016-0451-8.

Murillo-Barroso, M., Peñalver, E., Bueno P. et al. 2018. Amber in prehistoric Iberia: New data and a review. *PloS One* 13: e0202235. https://doi.org/10.1371/journal.pone.0202235.

Needham, S. 2005. Transforming Beaker culture in north-west Europe: Processes of fusion and fission. *Proceedings of the Prehistoric Society* 71: 171–217. https://doi.org/10.1017/S0079497X00001006.

Needham, S., Lawson, A. J., and Woodward, A. 2010. 'A noble group of barrows': Bush Barrow and the Normanton Down Early Bronze Age cemetery two centuries on. *The Antiquaries Journal* 90: 1–39. https://doi.org/10.1017/s0003581510000077.

Nekkal, F., and Mikdad, A. 2014. Quelques données sur la découverte de céramiques campaniformes au Maroc. *International Journal of Innovation and Applied Studies* 8: 632–638.

Nicolas, C. 2017. Arrows of power from Brittany to Denmark (2500–1700 BC). *Proceedings of the Prehistoric Society* 83: 247–287. https://doi.org/10.1017/ppr.2017.5.

Nicolas, C. 2020. Bracer Ornaments! An investigation of Bell Beaker stone 'wrist-guards' from Central Europe. *Journal of Neolithic Archaeology* 22: 15–107. https://doi.org/10.12766/jna.2020.2.

Nicolas, C., Favrel, Q., Rousseau, L. et al. 2019. The introduction of the Bell Beaker culture in Atlantic France: An overview of settlements. In Gibson, A., ed., *The Bell Beaker Settlement of Europe: The Bell Beaker Phenomenon from a Domestic Perspective*. Oxford: Oxbow Books: 329–352.

Nicolis, F., ed., 2001. *Bell Beakers Today: Pottery, People, Culture, Symbols in Prehistoric Europe*. Trento: Ufficio Beni Archeologici.

Noble, G., Brophy, K., Hamilton, D., Leach, S., and Sheridan, A. 2017. Cremation practices and the creation of monument complexes: The Neolithic cremation cemetery at Forteviot, Strathearn, Perth & Kinross, Scotland, and its comparanda. *Proceedings of the Prehistoric Society* 83: 213–245. https://doi.org/10.1017/ppr.2017.11.

Nocete, F., Vargas, J. M., Schuhmacher, T. X., Banerjee, A., and Dindorf, W. 2013. The ivory workshop of Valencina de la Concepción (Seville, Spain) and the identification of ivory from Asian elephant on the Iberian Peninsula in the first half of the 3rd millennium BC. *Journal of Archaeological Science* 40: 1579–1592. https://doi.org/10.1016/j.jas.2012.10.028.

O'Brien, W. 2004. *Ross Island: Mining, Metal and Society in Early Ireland*. Galway: National University of Ireland.

Olalde, I., Brace, S., Allentoft, M. E. et al. 2018. The Beaker phenomenon and the genomic transformation of northwest Europe. *Nature* 555: 190–196. https://doi.org/10.1038/nature25738.

Olalde, I. Mallick, S., Patterson, N. et al. 2019. The genomic history of the Iberian Peninsula over the past 8000 years. *Science* 363: 1230–1234. https://doi.org/10.1126/science.aav4040.

Ortega, L. A., Alonso-Fernández, C., Guede, I. et al. 2021. Strontium and oxygen isotopes to trace mobility routes during the Bell Beaker period in the north of Spain. *Scientific Reports* 11: 19553. https://doi.org/10.1038/s41598-021-99002-8.

Ovaskainen, O., and Saastamoinen, M. 2018. Frontiers in metapopulation biology: The legacy of Ilkka Hanski. *Annual Review of Ecology, Evolution, and Systematics* 49: 231–252. https://doi.org/10.1146/annurev-ecolsys-110617-062519.

Papac, L., Ernée, M., Dobeš, M. et al. 2021. Dynamic changes in genomic and social structures in third millennium BCE central Europe. *Science Advances* 7: 35. https://doi.org/10.1126/sciadv.abi6941.

Parker Pearson, M. P. 2019. *The Beaker People: Isotopes, Mobility and Diet in Prehistoric Britain*. Oxford: Oxbow Books.

Parker Pearson, M., Chamberlain, A., Jay, M. et al. 2009. Who was buried at Stonehenge? *Antiquity* 83: 23–39. https://doi.org/10.1017/s0003598x00098069.

Patterson, N., Isakov, M., Booth, T. et al. 2021. Large-scale migration into Britain during the Middle to Late Bronze Age. *Nature* 601: 588–594. https://doi.org/10.1038/s41586-021-04287-4.

Pétrequin, P. 1993. North wind, south wind: Neolithic technical choices in the Jura mountains, 3700-2400 BC. In Lemonnier, P., ed., *Technological choices: Transformation in Material Cultures since the Neolithic*. London: Routledge: 36–76.

Pétrequin, P., Cassen, S., Errera, M. et al., eds., 2012. *JADE. Grandes haches alpines du Néolithique européen. Ve et IVe millénaires av. J.-C.* Besançon: Presses Universitaires de Franche-Comté.

Petřík, J., Sosna, D., Prokeě L., Štefanisko, D., and Galeta, P. 2018. Shape matters: Assessing regional variation of Bell Beaker projectile points in Central Europe using geometric morphometrics. *Archaeological and Anthropological Sciences* 10: 893–904. https://doi.org/10.1007/s12520-016-0423-z.

Prescott, C. 2020. Interpreting complex diachronic 'Neolithic'-period data in Norway. In Gron K. J., Sørensen L., and Rowley-Conwy P., eds., *Farmers at the Frontier: A Pan-European Perspective on Neolithisation*. Oxford: Oxbow Books: 381–400.

Price, T. D., Knipper, C., Grupe, G., and Smrcka, V. 2004. Strontium isotopes and prehistoric human migration: The Bell Beaker period in central Europe. *European Journal of Archaeology* 7: 9–40. https://doi.org/10.1177/1461957104047992.

Price, T. D., Grupe, G., and Schröter, P. 1998. Migration in the Bell Beaker period of central Europe. *Antiquity* 72: 405–411. https://doi.org/10.1017/S0003598X00086683.

Priego, M. C. and Quero, S. 1992. *El Ventorro, un poblado prehistórico de los albores de la metalurgia*. Madrid: Ayuntamiento de Madrid, Estudios de Prehistoria y Arqueología Madrileñas.

Prieto-Martínez, M. P. 2019. Settlement in the north-west Iberian Peninsula in the 3rd and 2nd millennia BC. In Gibson, A., ed., *The Bell Beaker Settlement of Europe: The Bell Beaker Phenomenon from a Domestic Perspective*. Oxford: Oxbow Books: 25–43.

Prieto-Martinez, M. P., and Salanova, L. 2009. Coquilles et Campaniforme en Galice et en Bretagne: mécanismes de circulation et stratégies identitaires. *Bulletin de la Société préhistorique française* 106: 73–93. https://doi.org/10.3406/bspf.2009.13830.

Racimo, F., Woodbridge, J., Fyfe, R. et al. 2020. The spatiotemporal spread of human migrations during the European Holocene. *PNAS* 117: 8989–9000. https://doi.org/10.1073/pnas.1920051117.

Reimer, P. J., Austin, W. E., Bard, E. et al. 2020. The IntCal20 Northern Hemisphere radiocarbon age calibration curve (0–55 cal kBP). *Radiocarbon* 62: 725–757. https://doi.org/10.1017/RDC.2020.41.

Reményi, L., Endrödi, A., Gyulai, F., and Biró, K. T. 2019. Houses and settlements of the Bell Beaker groups in the Carpathian basin: cultural and economic contexts. In Gibson, A., ed., *The Bell Beaker Settlement of Europe: The Bell Beaker Phenomenon from a Domestic Perspective*. Oxford: Oxbow Books: 217–234.

Remicourt, M., Saintot, S., and Rey, P.-J. 2018. Les armatures à encoches latérales et à encoches basilaires à la fin du Néolithique, des Alpes à la façade atlantique. *Bulletin de la Société Préhistorique Française* 115: 125-147. https://doi.org/10.3406/bspf.2018.14863.

Risch, R., Friederich, S., Küssner, M., and Meller, H. 2022. Architecture and settlement dynamics in central Germany from the Late Neolithic to the Early Bronze Age. *Proceedings of the Prehistoric Society* 88: 123–154. https://doi.org/10.1017/ppr.2022.10.

Rivollat, M., Mendisco, F., Pemonge, M. H. et al. 2015. When the waves of European Neolithization met: First paleogenetic evidence from early farmers in the southern Paris Basin. *PloS One* 10: e0125521. https://doi.org/10.1371/journal.pone.0125521.

Roberts B. W., and Vander Linden M. 2011. Introduction. In Roberts B., and Vander Linden M., eds., *Investigating Archaeological Cultures: Material Culture Variability and Transmission*. New-York: Springer: 1–21.

Roberts, B. W., Thornton, C. P., and Pigott, V. C. 2009. Development of metallurgy in Eurasia. *Antiquity* 83: 1012–1022. https://doi.org/10.1017/s0003598x00099312.

Rojo-Guerra, M. Á., Garrido-Pena, R., García-Martínez-de-Lagrán Í. , Juan-Tresseras, J., and Matamala J. C. 2006. Beer and Bell Beakers: Drinking rituals in Copper Age inner Iberia. *Proceedings of the Prehistoric Society* 72: 243–265. https://doi.org/10.1017/s0079497x00000840.

Saag, L., Varul, L., Scheib, C. et al. 2017. Extensive farming in Estonia started through a sex-biased migration from the Steppe. *Current Biology* 27: 2185–2193. https://doi.org/10.1016/j.cub.2017.06.022.

Salanova, L. 1998. Le statut des assemblages campaniformes en contexte funéraire: la notion de 'bien de prestige'. *Bulletin de la Société préhistorique française* 95: 315–326. https://doi.org/10.3406/bspf.1998.10806.

Salanova, L. 2000. *La Question du Campaniforme en France et dans les îles anglo–normandes. Productions, chronologie et rôles d'un standard céramique*. Paris: C.T.H.S./Société Préhistorique Française.

Salanova, L. 2011. Chronologie et facteurs d'évolution des sépultures individuelles campaniformes dans le Nord de la France. In Salanova, L., and Tchérémissinoff, Y., eds., *Les sépultures individuelles campaniformes en France*. Paris: CNRS Éditions: 125–142. https://doi.org/10.4000/books.editionscnrs.55110.

Salanova, L., Brunet, P., Cottiaux, R. et al. 2011. Du Néolithique récent à l'âge du Bronze dans le Centre Nord de la France: les étapes de l'évolution chrono-culturelle. *Revue Archéologique de Picardie* 28: 77–101 . https://doi.org/10.3406/pica.2011.3323.

Salanova, L., Renard, C., and Mille B. 2011. Réexamen du mobilier de la sépulture campaniforme d'Arenberg, Wallers (Nord). In Salanova, L., and Tchérémissinoff, Y., eds., *Les sépultures individuelles campaniformes en France*. Paris: CNRS Éditions: 79–95. https://doi.org/10.4000/books.editionscnrs.55055.

Salanova, L., Prieto-Martinez, P., Clop-Garcia, X. et al. 2016. What are large-scale Archaeometric programmes for? Bell Beaker pottery and societies from the third millennium BC in Western Europe: Bell Beaker pottery and societies in western Europe. *Archaeometry* 58: 722–735. https://doi.org/10.1111/arcm.12173.

Salavert, A., Zazzo, A., Martin, L. et al. 2020. Direct dating reveals the early history of opium poppy in western Europe. *Scientific Reports* 10: 20263. https://doi.org/10.1038/s41598-020-76924-3.

Sample, C., Fryxell, J. M., Bieri, J. A. et al. 2018. A general modeling framework for describing spatially structured population dynamics. *Ecology and Evolution* 8: 493–508. https://doi.org/10.1002/ece3.3685.

Sangmeister, E. 1966. Die Datierung des Rückstroms der Glockenbecher und ihreAuswirkung auf die Chronologie der Kupferzeit in Portugal. *Palaeohistoria* 12: 195–207.

Sarauw, T. 2007. Male symbols or warrior identities? The 'archery burials' of the Danish Bell Beaker culture. *Journal of Anthropological Archaeology* 26: 65–87. https://doi.org/10.1016/j.jaa.2006.05.001.

Sarauw, T. 2019. Bell Beaker settlements in Denmark. In Gibson, A., ed., *The Bell Beaker Settlement of Europe: The Bell Beaker Phenomenon from a Domestic Perspective*. Oxford: Oxbow Books: 277–294.

Sarti, L., Fenu, P., Leonini, V., Martini, F., and Perusin, S. 2012. The Bell Beaker Tumulus of Via Bruschi in Sesto Fiorentino (Florence, Italy): New Research. In Borgna, E., and Müller Celka, S., eds., *Ancestral Landscape:*

Burial Mounds in the Copper and Bronze Ages (Central and Eastern Europe – Balkans – Adriatic – Aegean, 4th-2nd Millinneium B.C.). Lyon: Maison de l'Orient: 231–238.

Saupe, T., Montinaro, F., Scaggion, G. et al. 2021. Ancient genomes reveal structural shifts after the arrival of Steppe-related ancestry in the Italian Peninsula. *Current Biology* 31: 2576–2591. https://doi.org/10.1016/j.cub.2021.04.022.

Schuhmacher, T. X., Cardoso, J. L., and Banerjee, A. 2009. Sourcing African ivory in Chalcolithic Portugal. *Antiquity* 83: 983–997. https://doi.org/10.1017/s0003598x00099294.

Seguin-Orlando, A., Donat, R., Der Sarkissian, C. et al. 2021. Heterogeneous hunter-gatherer and Steppe-related ancestries in Late Neolithic and Bell Beaker genomes from present-day France. *Current Biology* 31: 1072–1083. https://doi.org/10.1016/j.cub.2020.12.015.

Shennan, S. J. 1976. Bell Beakers and their context in central Europe. In Lanting, J. N., and van der Waals, J. D., eds., *Glockenbecher Symposion: Oberried (1974)*. Haarlem: Fibula-Van Dishoeck: 231–239.

Shennan, S. J. 1978. Archaeological 'cultures': An empirical investigation. In Hodder, I., ed., *The Spatial Organisation of Culture*. London: Duckworth: 113–140.

Shennan, S. J. 1986. Central Europe in the third millennium B.C.: An evolutionary trajectory for the beginning of the European Bronze Age. *Journal of Anthropological Archaeology* 5: 115–146. https://doi.org/10.1016/0278-4165(86)90011-5.

Shennan, S. J. 1993. Settlement and social change in central Europe, 3500-1500 BC. *Journal of World Prehistory* 7: 121–161.

Shepherd, A. 2012. Stepping out together: Men, women and their Beakers in time and space. In Allen, M. J., Gardiner, J., and Sheridan, J. A., eds., *Is There a British Chalcolithic? People, Place and Polity in the Late 3rd Millennium*, 257–80. Oxford: Prehistoric Society Research Paper 4.

Sherratt, A. G. 1981. Plough and pastoralism: Aspects of the secondary products revolution. In Hodder, I., Isaac, G., and Hammond, N., eds., *Pattern of the Past*. Cambridge: Cambridge University Press: 261–306.

Sherratt, A. G. 1987. Cups that cheered. In Waldren, W. H., and Kennard, R. C., eds., *Bell Beakers of the Western Mediterranean, British Archaeological Reports (International Series)*, *331*. Oxford: Archaeopress: 81–114.

Simonsen, J. 2018. Beaker longhouses: Livelihood specialization and settlement continuity in North Jutland. *Journal of Neolithic Archaeology* 4: 161–184. https://doi.org/10.12766/jna.2018S.9.

Sjögren, K.-G., Olalde, I., Carver, S. et al. 2020. Kinship and social organization in Copper Age Europe. A cross-disciplinary analysis of archaeology, DNA, isotopes, and anthropology from two Bell Beaker cemeteries. *PloS One* 15: e0241278. https://doi.org/10.1371/journal.pone.0241278.

Solheim, S. 2021. Timing the emergence and development of arable farming in southeastern Norway by using summed probability distribution of radiocarbon dates and a Bayesian age model. *Radiocarbon* 63: 1503–1524. https://doi.org/10.1017/RDC.2021.80.

Soriano, I., Herrero-Corral, A. M., Garrido-Pena, R., and Majó, T. 2021. Sex/gender system and social hierarchization in Bell Beaker burials from Iberia. *Journal of Anthropological Archaeology* 64: 1013–1035. https://doi.org/10.1016/j.jaa.2021.101335.

Spatzier, A., and Bertemes, F. 2018. The ring sanctuary of Pömmelte, Germany: A monumental, multi-layered metaphor of the late third millennium BC. *Antiquity* 92: 655–673. https://doi.org/10.15184/aqy.2018.92.

Spatzier, A., and Schumke, T. 2019. Settlements and social development of the 3rd millennium BC in central Germany. In Gibson, A., ed., *The Bell Beaker Settlement of Europe: The Bell Beaker Phenomenon from a Domestic Perspective*. Oxford: Oxbow Books: 235–254.

Stevens, C. J., and Fuller, D. Q. 2012. Did Neolithic farming fail? The case for a Bronze Age agricultural revolution in the British Isles. *Antiquity* 86: 707–722. https://doi.org/10.1017/s0003598x00047864.

Strahm, C. 2019. Bell Beaker settlements in central Germany. In Gibson, A., ed., *The Bell Beaker Settlement of Europe: The Bell Beaker Phenomenon from a Domestic Perspective*. Oxford: Oxbow Books: 165–175.

Sweeney, L., Harrison, S. P., and Vander Linden, M. 2022. Assessing anthropogenic influence on fire history during the Holocene in the Iberian Peninsula. *Quaternary Science Reviews* 287: 107562. https://doi.org/10.1016/j.quascirev.2022.107562.

Tchérémissinoff, Y., Convertini, F., Fouéré, P., and Salanova, L. 2011. La sépulture campaniforme de La Folie, Poitiers (Vienne). In Salanova, L., and Tchérémissinoff, Y., eds., *Les sépultures individuelles campaniformes en France*. Paris: CNRS Éditions: 11–19. https://doi.org/10.4000/books.editionscnrs.54950.

Thomas, J. 2010. The return of the Rinyo-Clacton folk? The cultural significance of the Grooved Ware complex in later Neolithic Britain. *Cambridge Archaeological Journal* 20: 1–15. https://doi.org/10.1017/S0959774310000016.

Tinévez, J.-Y. 2022. L'habitat néolithique en Bretagne: un bilan des recherches, 1999-2018. *Revue Archéologique de l'Ouest* 38. https://doi.org/10.4000/rao.8024.

Towers, J., Montgomery, J., Evans, J., Jay, M., and Parker Pearson M. P. 2010. An investigation of the origins of cattle and aurochs deposited in the Early Bronze Age barrows at Gayhurst and Irthlingborough. *Journal of Archaeological Science* 37: 508–515. https://doi.org/10.1016/j.jas.2009.10.012.

Turek, J. 2013. Age and gender identities in European Copper Age: An anthropological perspective. *Indian Anthropologist* 43: 73–86. http://www.jstor.org/stable/43858418.

Turek, J. 2019. Bohemia and Moravia – local and Beaker: Bell Beaker domestic sites in the context of the Late Eneolithic/Early Bronze Age cultural sequence. In Gibson, A., ed., *The Bell Beaker Settlement of Europe. The Bell Beaker Phenomenon from a Domestic Perspective*. Oxford: Oxbow Books: 195–215.

Valera, A. C., Mataloto, R., and Basílio, A. C. 2019. The South Portugal perspective: Beaker sites or sites with Beakers. In Gibson, A., ed., *The Bell Beaker Settlement of Europe: The Bell Beaker Phenomenon from a Domestic Perspective*. Oxford: Oxbow Books: 1–23.

Valera, A. C., Žalaitė, I., Maurer, A. F. et al. 2020. Addressing human mobility in Iberian Neolithic and Chalcolithic ditched enclosures: The case of Perdigões (South Portugal). *Journal of Archaeological Science: Reports* 30: 102264. https://doi.org/10.1016/j.jasrep.2020.102264.

Vander Linden, M. 2006. *Le phénomène campaniforme dans l'Europe du 3ème millénaire avant notre ère: synthèse et nouvelles perspectives. British Archaeological International Series 1470*. Oxford: Archaeopress.

Vander Linden, M. 2007. What linked the Bell Beakers in third millennium BC Europe? *Antiquity* 81: 343–52. https://doi.org/10.1017/S0003598X00095223.

van der Waals, J. D., and Glasbergen, W. 1955. Beaker types and their distribution in the Netherlands; intrusive types, mutual influences and local evolutions. *Palaeohistoria* 4: 5–46.

Vander Linden, M. 2016. Population history in third-millennium-BC Europe: Assessing the contribution of genetics. *World Archaeology* 48: 714–728. https://doi.org/10.1080/00438243.2016.1209124.

Villalba-Mouco, V., Oliart, C., Rihuete-Herrada-, C. et al. 2021. Genomic transformation and social organization during the Copper Age-Bronze Age transition in southern Iberia. *Science Advances* 7: eabi7038. https://doi.org/10.1126/sciadv.abi7038.

Všianský, D., Kolář, J., and Petřík, J. 2014. Continuity and changes of manufacturing traditions of Bell Beaker and Bronze Age encrusted pottery in the Morava river catchment (Czech Republic). *Journal of Archaeological Science* 49: 414–422. https://doi.org/10.1016/j.jas.2014.05.028.

Waterman, A. J., Peate, D. W., Silva, A. M., and Thomas, J. T. 2014. In search of homelands: Using strontium isotopes to identify biological markers of mobility in late prehistoric Portugal. *Journal of Archaeological Science* 42: 119–127. https://doi.org/10.1016/j.jas.2013.11.004.

Wentink, K. 2020. *Stereotype: The Role of Grave Sets in Corded Ware and Bell Beaker Funerary Practices*. Leiden: Sidestone Press.

Wilkin, N., and Vander Linden, M. 2015. What was and what would never be: Changing patterns of interaction and archaeological visibility across North West Europe from 2500 to 1500 calBC. In Anderson-Whymark, H., Garrow, D., and Sturt, F., eds., *Continental Connections: Exploring Cross-Channel Relationships from the Mesolithic to the Iron Age*. Oxford: Oxbow Books: 99–121.

Woodward, A., Hunter, J., Ixer, R. et al. 2006. Beaker age bracers in England: Sources, function and use. *Antiquity* 80: 530–43. https://doi.org/10.1017/S0003598X00094011.

Woodward, A., Hunter, J., Bukach, D. et al. 2011. *An Examination of Prehistoric Stone Bracers from Britain: An Examination of Prehistoric Stone Bracers from Britain*. Oxford: Oxbow Books. https://doi.org/10.2307/j.ctv13pk810.

Wright, E., Waterman, A. J., Peate, D. W. et al. 2019. Animal mobility in Chalcolithic Portugal: Isotopic analyses of cattle from the sites of Zambujal and Leceia. *Journal of Archaeological Science: Reports* 24: 804–814. https://doi.org/10.1016/j.jasrep.2019.02.005.

Zilhão, J., Monge Soares, A. M., and Gonçalves, A. P. 2022. Botones de cachalote con perforación en V de Galeria da Cisterna (Sistema Kárstico de Almonda, Torres Novas, Portugal). *Trabajos de Prehistoria* 79: 131–140. https://doi.org/10.3989/tp.2022.12291.

Acknowledgements

Over the past two decades, my trajectory has not only involved crossing the North Sea but also journeying across several institutions, and building a network of contacts with colleagues across Europe and beyond. It is impossible for me to name all the outstanding individuals who, at some point and in varying capacity, have been kind enough to listen to me, and to speak to me. Though bound to forget several names, I would thus like to take the opportunity to thank: David Meltzer, Erick Robinson, Jacob Freeman, Nicki Whitehouse, Andrew Fitzpatrick, Ben Roberts, Niels Njørkær Johannsen, Martin Furholt, Dani Hoffmann, Colin Haselgrove, Mike Parker Pearson, Kevan Edinborough, Stephen Shennan, Cyprian Broodbank, Sue Hakenbeck, Paul Lane, Chris Evans, Cameron Petrie, Enrico Crema, Maja Gori, Andrea DiRenzoni, Giulio Lucarini, Johan Ling, Christian Horn, Jean-Pierre Bocquet-Appel†, David Orton, Aitor Ruiz-Redondo, Ivana Jovanović, Sébastien Manem, Jane Gaastra, Anne de Vareilles, and Nelis Drost. In March 2022, I joined the Institute for Modelling of Socio-Environmental Transitions at Bournemouth University, and I would like to thank my colleagues there who, perhaps more than they realise it, have had a positive impact upon my career: Adrian Newton, Kim Davies, Fiona Coward, Phil Riris, Emma Jenkins, and Fabio Silva. Extra special thanks to Mark Gillings for being kind enough to read and comment upon the first draft of this manuscript. Lastly, extra thanks are due to Manuel Fernandez-Gotz for inviting and trusting me to deliver this little opus.

Becoming a migrant also shaped my personal life in the most unexpected, long-lasting, and blossoming way. In this sense, this little element would not have seen the light without that experience and without the support of my parents in letting me set myself free from the shackles of then unrewarding Belgian academia. But the most important thanks of all go to my children, Lili and Charly, for being so unique and for putting up with their father's commute and bad bilingual puns, and to my wife, Tamsin O'Connell, simply for everything she has ever offered to me.

Cambridge Elements ☰

The Archaeology of Europe

Manuel Fernández-Götz

University of Edinburgh

Manuel Fernández-Götz is Abercromby Professor of Archaeology at the University of Edinburgh. His research focuses on late prehistoric and Roman Europe, the archaeology of identities, and conflict archaeology. He has directed fieldwork projects in Spain, Germany, the United Kingdom, and Croatia. Between 2015–21 he was board member of European Association of Archaeologists.

Bettina Arnold

University of Wisconsin–Milwaukee

Bettina Arnold is a Full Professor of Anthropology at the University of Wisconsin–Milwaukee and Adjunct Curator of European Archaeology at the Milwaukee Public Museum. Her research interests include the archaeology of alcohol, the archaeology of gender, mortuary archaeology, Iron Age Europe and the history of archaeology.

About the Series

Elements in the Archaeology of Europe is a collaborative publishing venture between Cambridge University Press and the European Association of Archaeologists. Composed of concise, authoritative, and peer-reviewed studies by leading scholars, each volume in this series will provide timely, accurate, and accessible information about the latest research into the archaeology of Europe from the Paleolithic era onwards, as well as on heritage preservation.

E
A   European Association
A   *of* Archaeologists

Cambridge Elements ☰

The Archaeology of Europe

Printed in the United States
by Baker & Taylor Publisher Services